PERFECT
PHRASES

for

ESL

Advancing Your Career

**Hundreds of Ready-to-Use Phrases
That Help You Speak Fluently,
Understand "Business Speak," Network
in the Global Workplace, Present
Confidently, and More**

Natalie Gast

New York   Chicago   San Francisco   Lisbon   London   Madrid   Mexico City
Milan   New Delhi   San Juan   Seoul   Singapore   Sydney   Toronto

Library of Congress Cataloging-in-Publication Data

Gast, Natalie.
    Perfect phrases for ESL : advancing your career / by Natalie Gast.
        p.   cm.
    ISBN-13: 978-0-07-160836-7
    1. English language— Study and teaching— Foreign speakers.   2. English
language— Terms and phrases.   I. Title.

    PE1128.G34   2010
    428.2'4—dc22   2009049803

  2 3 4 5 6 7 8 9 10 11 12 13 14 15   QFR/QFR   1 9 8 7 6 5 4 3 2 1

ISBN 978-0-07-160836-7
MHID   0-07-160836-2

McGraw-Hill books are available at special quantity discounts to use as premiums and
sales promotions or for use in corporate training programs. To contact a representative,
please e-mail us at bulksales@mcgraw-hill.com.

Contents

Part 1 Getting Down to Business   1

Part 2 The Written Word   39

Contents

Preface

Who Can Benefit from Using This Book?

Perfect Phrases for ESL: Advancing Your Career has been created for intermediate and advanced level English as a second language (ESL) or English as a foreign language (EFL) learners already in—or planning to be in—the workforce in the United States. If you are presently employed, you will find that you always need to refine and improve your skills—since the one constant of the business world is change! This book helps you reinforce the skills you have in order to be more valuable to your employer—in such areas as communicating with colleagues, leading meetings and teams, making presentations, representing your company, or supervising others.

And if you are presently employed, you may be applying for other work within your company. The position you are applying for may be a **step up the ladder** in the department in which you now work, or it may be a **lateral move** to another department within your company. Conversely, you may feel that you have reached the highest level you can in your present company. Therefore, you may want to consider a job search in other corporate or industrial settings. Another possibility you may be thinking about is to try to start your own business.

Whatever the scenario, your ability to communicate confidently will be crucial.

Whatever your choice is in the world of work, the phrases in this book will be of help to you. You may take the phrases as they are presented and memorize them for use, or you may make changes to them to fit your own situation and put them in your own words for practice. You might also adapt the phrases to other conditions and situations. You could also benefit from the use of these phrases in other areas of your life. Your confidence in using American English in job- and job-search-related situations will increase as you practice by yourself, with friends and colleagues, and finally "**taking it on the road**" in real work-related areas such as interviews, meetings, and dealing with conflicts.

You may already have read *Perfect Phrases for ESL: Everyday Business Life*, the first *Perfect Phrases* book developed for the English as a second language audience by McGraw-Hill Professional. *Perfect Phrases for ESL: Advancing Your Career* may be used as a companion text to that book, but it also stands alone. The phrases and the situations in which to utilize them are different in each volume. Look over the table of contents for each book to determine which one meets your needs—or perhaps both books will have phrases you find useful.

How to Use This Book

Perfect Phrases for ESL: Advancing Your Career is presented in five parts that focus on different areas of career development, with each part containing four or five chapters. You may choose to start at the beginning of the book and read through to the end. This is an especially good method if you are not yet seeking employment or are preparing to come to the United States for prearranged employment. This enables you to **bone up** on the idioms and vocabulary as well as **get a flavor of** some aspects of business in the United States.

The beginning-to-end method also works well if you have been working in the United States and are about to **embark** on a new job search campaign, whether inside your present company or in a **new territory**.

You may want to refer to *Perfect Phrases for ESL: Advancing Your Career* on an **as-needed basis**. For example, a business conflict may arise, your résumé might need reworking, you may be preparing for an interview, meetings may leave your **head spinning**, or any number of circumstances may occur that are addressed by a specific chapter. Perhaps just reading a chapter could direct you to further information in the library or on the Internet.

This text is designed for you to write notes on the pages following each Part. **Take the liberty** to connect with the book: underline or highlight sections, **dog-ear** pages, and attach **Post-it notes**. Use whatever techniques help you to reinforce material when learning a language.

Everybody learns differently: some learn by writing things over many times, some by hearing the information spoken (you may record sections or ask an English-speaking friend or colleague to do so); others learn by reading out loud or even by being read to. Find which techniques work for you and use them.

The book fits into a briefcase or **purse**, which makes it easy to take with you and use while traveling by public transportation, waiting for an appointment, or eating lunch alone. It may also serve as a conversation starter or icebreaker. If you and a friend each have a copy of the book, you may brainstorm about how to use the phrases that are listed in the book or your own phrases. Experiment, **venture forth** into "safe" situations with original phrases you develop. **Gauge** reactions from others in these nonthreatening places, and you will gain confidence. Another productive and fun way to use this book is in a group with other English as a second language (ESL) learners. They will probably bring their own experiences and cultural backgrounds to the mix. It can also act as a **jumping-off point** for a study group where you meet new people and make new friends as well as learn.

Idioms and Other Vocabulary

As-needed basis: finding out or getting only what you need at the time

Bone up: study a subject

Dog-ear: to turn down the corner of a page to mark a place in a book

Embark: start, begin

Gauge: make a judgment about

Get a flavor of: get an idea of

Head spinning: confused, excited, overwhelmed

Jumping-off point: a place to start

Lateral move: a move to a different job, but on the same level within a company

New territory: a place or situation you haven't been in before

Purse: a cloth or leather bag used to hold papers, money, and other necessities, also called a *pocketbook* or *handbag*

Post-it notes: the trademark name for a small piece of sticky paper, used for notes

Step up the ladder: advancement in your career

Take the liberty: feel free to; you may do this

Taking it on the road: using it elsewhere

Venture forth: go and attempt something

Acknowledgments

I am most grateful to Harriet Diamond, my sister, who has written several *Perfect Phrases* books for McGraw-Hill Professional. In addition to understanding the publishing business, Harriet has been—and continues to be—a most active inspiration to me; she has made this venture possible.

Walter Ladden, my companion, is still the best proofreader I know; he has read every word of this book, some words many times. His exceptional English language skills and his expertise in sports- and business-related terms were invaluable in creating this book.

All of my friends have been there for me by respecting my time constraints and recent restricted accessibility. They speak to me now in "perfect phrases"! Gail Dunigan drove 600 miles from New Mexico to meet me in California, where I was for a special event. There, she shared her own unique ESL experiences and suggestions.

Support staff is crucial in completing a book project, as my niece, Ellen Diamond, who ably assisted in this respect, demonstrated. Maxine Lipp, my friend and owner of Baron Personnel, came through by sharing the capable and overqualified Joanne Goodford. Gail Gallagher, my former office manager and a Mac computer genius, had weekend duty. Andi Jeszenszky, my administrative assistant, who is now completing her master's degree in business administration, was generous with her limited time and her unlimited skills.

Acknowledgments

Grace Freedson, my trusted agent, led me to McGraw-Hill Professional, where Holly McGuire, my editor, offered valuable suggestions and acted as a professional cheerleader. Tama Harris McPhatter, production supervisor, came through with final reassurances.

This book is dedicated to all of the English-as-a-second-language (ESL) learners who appear in these pages under made-up names and dance through my head with their actual names. I will never forget what these people have taught me about my craft. They have also shown me how similar all people are, and where they differ from one another, how these differences need to be respected. I hope that my trainees are able to make good use of what I taught them.

Part 1

Getting Down to Business

"Not **Indispensable**, Perhaps, But Valuable"

When I worked at a college, I placed students in jobs as well as taught them ESL. I helped Myung Soo Park get his first job in a fast-food restaurant. A few weeks after the placement, I received a phone call from the manager of the fast-food chain. He said, "Can you send me another Mike?" I asked, "Who's Mike?" He said, "The guy you sent two weeks ago; he's a **dynamo**. No one can say his name, so we call him Mike." I answered, "I'll do my best, but Myung Soo Park is a **hard act to follow** no matter what he allows you to call him." I found another student to work at the restaurant, but he was only half a Mike.

Myung has **kept in touch** with me for over thirty years and still sends me a Christmas card every year reporting on his progress and inquiring about mine. His card is always the first of the season, and I look forward to it very much. He got his next job himself at a major oil company. There was a large **layoff** at the company after Myung had worked there for several years, and I asked him why he thought he was not let go. His answer to me was that he had learned how to do everything—every task—at the company. He could wash the trucks, fuel the trucks, drive the trucks, fix the trucks, and **so forth**. He never felt that any job was **beyond or beneath** him. Although Myung tells me in every Christmas card how much he learned from me, I think that I learned more from him.

Chapter 1

You and Your Attitude at Work

Whether it's your first job or your tenth, whether you are just entering the world of work or making a career change, you are now concentrating on business behaviors. Whether you just arrived in the United States and need to **transfer skills** to a new country and, perhaps, a new career; or you've been here for many years and you've been laid off, or your industry has changed or has **dried up** due to technology or **downsizing**, you are now focusing on career issues such as keeping your job, getting new work, communicating about work, settling conflicts, and managing your time. Certain behaviors and attitudes can help you perform in your job, move up within your present workplace, or plan and proceed to a new **field** or career.

Your attitude is, perhaps, the **key factor** that determines what you make of your work environment. Attitude is simply the way you view things, circumstances, and people. Your attitude toward others **influences** your actions. You cannot **disguise** how you feel; it will be **reflected** in what you say, how you say it, and in many **nonverbal** ways.

Your attitude is not **fixed**. You can choose to display a positive or a negative attitude. You may also **elect** to change your attitude as you become better acquainted with your work surroundings, become skilled in the tasks required for you to do your job, and interact with your colleagues. In other words, you are able to make an **attitude adjustment**.

"What you give is what you get" is a basic rule of attitude. The attitude you send out to other people is usually the attitude you get back from them. If your attitude screams "**unapproachable**" or "I need to depend on everyone because I'm **insecure** here," you have created a negative situation—but you can change it to a positive situation with an attitude adjustment.

Those around you will never know exactly what your attitude is toward them, unless you choose to tell them, but they do make judgments about your attitude based on what they see and hear—your actions, your facial expressions, your listening style, and your **subsequent** actions. Projecting a positive attitude is a combination of many different factors including your body language, choice of words, tone of voice, and, of course, your behavior.

Attitudinal Phrases—Positive Feelings

It makes me feel good when others _____ (respect me / compliment me / seek me out / ask for my advice / ask for my opinions).

I'm glad that they want me to join them.

*I respond **constructively** when others _____ (ask for advice / ask me to solve problems / **solicit advice** from me).*

*I appreciate being included in a **decision-making process**.*

*I respect others when they _____ (respect me / are **courteous** / **follow through** on promises / **meet deadlines**).*

*I accept that others need to be treated with the same respect I **expect** for myself.*

*I understand that others need to **be true to their own values**.*

I am proud of my team. They _____ (work so well together / come up with really good suggestions / won the award last month).

Attitudinal Phrases—Negative Feelings

I find it difficult to tell others that they are _____ (wrong / too late / misinformed / fired / laid off / not performing their work well).

*It makes me angry when people _____ (yell / scream / act **belligerently** / act **arrogantly** / think they know it all / **get in my face**).*

*I feel hurt when others _____ (exclude me from conversations / **snub** me / think I can't **cope**).*

It's painful to me when others think I cannot do my work well because my English isn't perfect.

*Are you worried that the HR Department wants to see your **admin** today? The department called him to _____ (discuss his work record / check his **H1 visa** status / talk about his attendance).*

*I find it **frustrating** when others _____ (don't hear me / don't understand my English / don't care enough about what I am saying to ask me to clarify when they don't understand me / ask me to repeat many times / speak loudly as if I had difficulty hearing or was hard of hearing).*

Idioms and Other Vocabulary

Admin: short term for administrative assistant

Arrogantly: behaving as if one is better than, knows more than, or is superior to others

Attitude adjustment: change one's thinking or perspective

Be true to their values: follow what they believe in

Belligerently: in a way that is aggressively angry or hostile

Beyond or beneath: *beyond* means too difficult for him or her, and *beneath* means not good enough for him or her

Constructively: helpfully

Cope: handle, take care of, deal with

Courteous: polite

Decision-making process: a series of steps by which decisions are made

Disguise: make seem different, hide

Downsizing: reducing staff, production, or operations of a business

Dried up: came to an end

Dynamo: an energetic person

Elect: choose

Expect: look for, anticipate

Field: area of work

Fixed: not able to be changed

Follow through: complete, carry out

Frustrating: making one feel annoyed, upset, and impatient because one cannot get or do something one wants

Get in my face: persistently annoy me, be confrontational

Hard act to follow: so good that it would be difficult to find another as good

H1 visa: temporary visa to do specialized work

Indispensable: so important that it is impossible to get along without

Influences: has an effect on

Insecure: not feeling confident or comfortable

Kept in touch: stayed in contact

Key factor: main or most important influence

Layoff: stop in employment due to lack of work

Mantras: commonly repeated important words or phrases; originally from Buddhism and Hinduism

Meet deadlines: complete work on time

Nonverbal: not spoken

Reflected: seen in, evidenced in

Snub: to treat someone rudely, especially by ignoring him or her

So forth: more of the same

Solicit advice: ask for advice

Strive: make a great effort to do

Subsequent: occurring after

Transfer skills: move skills you have developed to a new location or a different career

Unapproachable: not friendly

Culture Hint: In the United States, a positive attitude is preferred, even if one doesn't feel very positive. "Keep your chin up" and "Pick yourself up, brush yourself off, and start all over again" are **mantras** that Americans **strive** to follow.

Grammar Notes: Adjectives, or descriptive words, have different endings depending on what is being described. If something that causes a feeling is being described, the -ing ending is often used. If the person's state of mind is being described, the -ed ending is often used.

For example, consider the adjectives frustrating and frustrated. Frustrating describes a situation that makes a person feel annoyed, upset, and impatient because of not being able to get or do something he or she wants: "It is frustrating when other people don't understand my English." Frustrated describes the state of mind in which a person is annoyed, upset, and impatient because of not being able to get or do something he or she wants: "I am frustrated when other people don't understand my English."

Boring and bored are also adjectives or descriptive words. Boring means not interesting: "This movie is boring." Bored describes the state of mind in which you are not interested in something: "I am bored by this movie."

Intimidating and intimidated are another useful pair. Intimidating describes the person or situation that makes someone feel worried, insecure, and not confident. Intimidated describes the state of mind of a person who feels worried, insecure, and not confident.

Other similar pairs of adjectives include interesting—interested, fascinating—fascinated, embarrassing—embarrassed, and exciting—excited.

Chapter 2

Becoming Indispensable

No one is truly indispensable; we see that over and over. It is a fact of life. However, you can become very valuable to your employer, and it is in your best interest to do so. You can work at learning skills that make you valuable to your company, your manager, your supervisor, your boss, or the small business owner who employs you. You can become such an **integral part** of the organization that no one will want to see you leave.

You increase your chances of surviving layoffs when times **get tough**, you increase your chances of surviving layoffs **in direct proportion to** how useful and **esteemed** you make yourself. You also increase your opportunity for gaining a promotion and/or a raise in salary. There are, of course, exceptions in downsizing as in everything else. Sometimes the **rule of thumb** is, **last hired, first fired**. The effort you make at becoming more useful and well thought of is not wasted, though, because you will get a more favorable recommendation and be better equipped to handle your next position.

You will be a valuable employee and will be given more responsibility if you are **versatile** and dependable. Colleagues will **rely upon** you and look up to you as well. You can become even more valuable by understanding how your work fits into the larger picture of the entire company's function, by learning additional skills and processes, by working cooperatively with others, and by communicating effectively.

Phrases for Making Yourself a More Valuable Employee—Offering Assistance

*I can see that you are **on overload**. How can I help?*

I'm free at the moment—how can I help?

Do you need me to tackle anything for you while you finish _____ (your presentation / the paperwork)?

*I can help you _____ (**reconcile that account** / put the proposal together / edit the company newsletter) if you are **pressed for time**.*

I know I can't help you develop your proposal, but I can help you by _____ (reacting to your ideas / proofreading / covering your phone so you can concentrate).

*Please consider me when you need help with _____ (picking up the supply order / filling out the forms / planning the new **product launch**).*

Would you like me to proofread your memo?

May I correct the meeting date in the memo you are about to send out? I know the date has been changed.

Please excuse the interruption, but the company vice president _____ (has arrived / is on line two / is in the conference room).

I think I can _____ (lead the meeting / train the new file clerk / cover for the teller during his break / pick up the order on my way into the factory).

What if we order these checks? They are half the price of the ones we are currently using.

Phrases for Making Yourself a More Valuable Employee—When You're Short-Staffed

I've heard that Juan is out sick today. How can I help you in his absence?

I don't mind handling that task.

I have a free hour tomorrow if you need me.

I noticed the filing is piling up. May I give it a try in my spare time?

May I clean out the storeroom? I'm good at organizing. I'll show you everything before disposing of anything.

If you want, I'll take a later lunch than the others so the phone is always covered.

*It seems the work in development _____ (is seasonal / has slowed down / is **winding down** for now); I'd be happy to go over to _____ (quality control / production / marketing / any other department) where they are **short on people** and _____ (learn / train / **shadow** someone / help out).*

Phrases for Making Yourself a More Valuable Employee—Training

*May I **shadow** you today when you take the monthly inventory? I can assist you and then be ready when you want me to do it myself.*

I just took an online course in _____ (accounting / business administration / Windows XP / Spanish / business law / principles of banking). Is there any way we can incorporate this into my job?

I took a class in _____ (PowerPoint presentations / using this software) before I came to the United States. Maybe it can be useful here.

I'd like to take advantage of the _____ (ESL / time management / organizational skills) training course being offered here next month.

*I see that there is a **Toastmasters** meeting during lunch on Thursdays. I think I could benefit by joining the group.*

There's a course in accounting for the _____ (pharmaceutical / food service / hospitality / health care) industry or _____ (manufacturing / retail sales / small business) at the college near here. I could go _____ (after work / two nights a week / on weekends).

*I could get some hands-on practice with what I learn during the course by _____ (**trying my hand at** new things here when things get slow / putting in some extra time in the departments that have downsized and need additional help).*

*_____ (I've never used / I haven't had a chance to use / I haven't taken) any of the educational credits we're _____ (allowed / **reimbursed for** / encouraged to take). I could do that now if you think there is a _____ (course / class / session) that _____ (I have a talent for / would be helpful for the company for me to study / might make me a more valuable employee).*

Idioms and Other Vocabulary

Arming: giving you support tools
Dedicated: committed to, focused on
End up: arrive at the finish or conclusion

Enrichment: improving quality by adding skills or knowledge

Esteemed: respected

Get tough: get difficult

In direct proportion to: in exact relationship to

Integral part: necessary for completeness

Last hired, first fired: the last person hired will be the first person fired if it becomes necessary to lay off people (due to having less **seniority**)

Motivated: wanting to achieve or accomplish something by working hard to do so

On overload: under pressure with excessive work

Pressed for time: under time pressure, not having enough time to complete necessary tasks

Product launch: introducing a new product

Reconcile the account: study the account to make sure it is correct

Reimbursed: you pay and the company pays you back

Rely upon: depend on

Rule of thumb: basic rule

Seniority: having worked at an organization for more time than another person or others

Short on people or short-staffed: not having enough people to do the work that needs to be done

Shadow: follow someone while he or she is performing a job in order to learn how the work is done

Toastmasters: an international public speaking group devoted to helping people improve their public speaking skills (a *toast* is raising a glass and saying nice things about a person or group, and a *master* is someone who excels at something)

Trying my hand at: attempting something new

Venue: place to have an activity

Versatile: good at doing many things and learning new things, sometimes called jack-of-all-trades
Wasted: of no use
Winding down: getting slower or decreasing

Culture Hints: *In the United States there are many ways to work. One of them is compartmentalization, in which an employee is trained to perform a specific task that is only one part of the whole project. That task becomes his or her* **dedicated** *job. An example of this is an assembly line in which a worker performs one task repeatedly. Another method, frequently found in smaller companies, offers the employee the opportunity to learn all aspects of the business or industry—in other words, to get the whole picture.*

In the United States, there are courses in every possible subject in every possible **venue**. *Some courses are for fun, some are for* **enrichment**, *and many are helpful for* **arming** *you with additional skills for the job market. These courses include creating business plans, improving managerial skills, computer training, presentation skills, public speaking, languages, English as a second language, business writing, and many others. Even if you don't* **end up** *using what you have learned at work, these courses are never* **wasted**. *You will learn new skills and meet new, interesting, and* **motivated** *people.*

Chapter 3

Time Management

Whether you work for a large or a small company, are in your own business, work in sales, or are involved in any other endeavor; managing your time—and sometimes others' time—is difficult and **crucial**. Everyone has his or her own approach to this challenging issue. Often, styles **clash**. If you like to have your schedule set early and your priorities clear, but you work for or with a creative **counterpart** who regularly comes to you with last minute "must dos" or "must haves," you need to balance **accommodating** this person with realistic expectations. If you're the last-minute type and you work with someone who's highly organized and **analytical**, you have a **learning curve** to master. Additionally, if you are a **big picture person** and don't work with a **detail person** who can **pick up the slack**, you may be in trouble. On the other hand, if you are a detail person without a big picture person to remind you of the larger goal, you could get **bogged down** in the **minutiae**.

There is always the unexpected. However, there are some protections that you can build in. Plan B is one of them. Plan B means that if your first plan—Plan A—doesn't work for whatever reason, you don't have to start figuring out what to do, whom to call, how to fix it. You have already done that in your head, on paper, or on the phone. You are **covered**. For example, suppose Steve is supposed to pick you up at 6 A.M. to drive to an important job that you are doing together, but Steve gets the stomach flu and can't do his part. If you checked **beforehand** with Joe to see if he is available as a substitute, you put the **scenario** in place in case an emergency arose. Whew! You are so glad to have backup, your Plan B.

Phrases to Help You Better Manage Your Time—Planning

Let's clarify our priorities. What must be _____ (accomplished / finished / worked on / started) _____ (today / this week / this month / before the meeting / before your vacation)?

Let's **map out a timeline**. That always helps me **put** all of my deadlines **in perspective**.

Can we meet to make a timeline?

What should be our top priority?

What is our **deadline**?

What do we have to accomplish before our deadline?

Can we meet to _____ (discuss my current workload / review the schedule / prepare a calendar)?

Let's review what we've done so far and look at the next steps.

What's your _____ (Plan B / backup / alternate plan / next step)?

Let's just focus on _____ (organizing the team meeting / the project / the current workload), and we can finish that and **cross it off**.

Ted is on vacation for two weeks, but we can still follow the **flowchart** in order to advance the project. He'll be happy we kept going.

*I know we have two weeks to complete this report, but let's get a **leg up**. Other distractions always come up.*

Phrases to Help You Better Manage Your Time—Buying Time

I'll work with you _____ (as soon as I finish this project / when I'm done working here / after lunch / later this morning / tomorrow).

I'd love to help you. I will as soon as . . .

Can we talk _____ (during my break / after my shift / tomorrow)?

I'm free tomorrow afternoon—can we meet then?

Why don't we slow down for a minute?

***Haste makes waste.** Let's not rush.*

*I'm sorry that my last-minute additions _____ (caused you problems / interrupted your **train of thought** / delayed the process).*

Phrases to Help You Better Manage Your Time—Saying No

*I'm sorry, I can't talk now; I'm _____ (**fighting a deadline** / late for a meeting / organizing a presentation).*

*I'd love to help you, but first I have to finish _____ (what I'm working on / what's on my list for today / what's **on my plate** / this item).*

I've got to say no: I have to meet my own deadline first. I'm sorry.

I know that I will have to _____ (work late / go to a marketing meeting / finish this report) on Wednesday. Could you pick up Mr. Kim at the airport?

I have so much on my plate that I don't think that I can _____ (attend your meeting / help you out / cover the phones / pick up that package).

*I would help with that _____ (**fund-raiser** / project / dinner) in a **New York minute** if only it were not _____ (next month / next week / in July).*

Idioms and Other Vocabulary

Accommodating: helpful, trying to do what others want

Agenda-less meetings: meetings without plans that lack direction

Analytical: using methods to examine and catalog information

At your fingertips: close by and convenient to use

Beforehand: before something else occurs

Big picture person: looking at something as a whole

Bogged down: stuck and not able to move

Bottom line: basic truth, most important fact

Clash: conflict

Counterpart: someone with the same job at another location or someone who works with you but in another way

Covered: taken care of; you have prepared for this

Crop up: happen suddenly

Cross it off: take if off the to-do list because it is done

Crucial: extremely important

Deadline: the final date when something has to be finished

Delegation: giving out parts of a job or jobs to others rather than doing everything yourself

Detail person: concerned with all the smaller separate parts of something

Fighting a deadline: struggling to finish something by the time it is due

Flexible: able to change and do things differently

Flowchart: a drawing of how the parts of a system are related or connected

Fund-raiser: an event planned to collect money for a particular purpose

Haste makes waste: going too quickly can cause mistakes that lead to problems

Learning curve: rate of speed at which you learn something new

Leg up: an advantage

Map out a timeline: make a plan about when things or events will happen

Minutiae: very small, unimportant details

New York minute: quick time; things in New York move fast

On my plate: scheduled for me to do

Pick up the slack: do some necessary work that was supposed to be done by someone else

Prioritizing: putting things in order of importance

Put something in perspective: evaluate it realistically

Scenario: a situation that could occur

Time wasters: less important things that take up valuable time

Train of thought: straight line of thinking about something

Two sides of a coin: two different features of the same idea

Zeroing in on: concentrating on

Culture Hint: *Working in American companies is often very competitive. The more skills you have* **at your fingertips,** *the more indispensable you become. Time management is a key organizational skill, and how you do it depends on your personal style and the demands of your company. There are* **two sides of a coin** *to time management. One side concerns planning, organization, and* **delegation.** *The other side is being* **flexible** *enough to act on sudden situations that* **crop up** *and need immediate attention. Here is where* **prioritizing** *and* **zeroing in on** *and eliminating* **time wasters** *come in. That is the* **bottom line.** *Issues that contribute to wasted time include lack of prioritizing, too many phone calls and/or e-mails, inability to say no to less important tasks, lack of focus, unnecessary and* **agenda-less meetings,** *and poor delegation skills.*

Chapter 4

Communication Is the Key

Communication is the best business tool anyone can have. Those who express themselves clearly and directly develop stronger working relationships and are more **effective** at any job. By speaking clearly—in both content and pronunciation—you will save time and avoid confusion. Also, by carefully communicating with others, you will avoid unnecessary misunderstandings, develop positive working relationships, and **position yourself** for greater achievement and opportunity.

The successful communicator is focused, comfortable, committed, knowledgeable, and has a **sense of humor**. He or she listens carefully to others and shows interest. This is demonstrated by making eye contact, asking well-chosen questions, responding, and following through appropriately. Each of these steps is necessary and cannot be **left to chance**. Eye contact is not staring without breaking the gaze, but looking someone in the eye, at his or her face. You may **glance** away now and then, but should not focus on the floor, the wall, or away from the speaker.

Showing interest includes making sure you understand what the person is saying by asking for **repetition**, clarification, demonstration, or even written help if necessary.

Comfort in communication comes with practice and exposure. There are a few people with whom we may never feel comfortable.

With most people, however, time and repeated exposure to the person's style and the **American way** of communicating in general help the process.

Phrases for Getting Information

I didn't hear you. Would you please _____ (turn to face me / not put your hand over your mouth / speak more loudly)?

Would you please say that again?

Would you please _____ (write that down / say that slowly)?

I really want to understand this. May I _____ (write it down / repeat it back to you / say it to you in other words / hear it again)?

I realize that you are _____ (upset / angry / in a hurry / confused by this), but I don't know why. Please slow down; I do want to understand what happened.

*Is the conference room _____ (room 212 / on the second floor / in this building or in the other building across the **courtyard**)?*

*I received the memo about Friday's meeting at 11 A.M. Do you want me to _____ (reserve the room **till** noon or longer / order lunch for the team / e-mail people to bring lunch with them)?*

The departmental report is due Tuesday. In order to include everyone's contribution, I must have them all by Friday at noon. I need time to _____ (type them / check the information / proofread / correct, print, and collate).

*Thank you for the client referral and phone number. Do you have an e-mail address as well? I prefer to e-mail before just calling **out of the blue**.*

This package must arrive in Detroit by tomorrow. What are my shipping options?

Sure, I can open attachments. Word is the easiest for us to deal with.

Sometimes people don't include their names in their e-mail addresses. I'd like to put your information in my address book so that your messages won't go to spam.

Phrases for Communicating with Colleagues/Coworkers

May I summarize _____ (your concern / the project / what I heard) as I understand it?

How do you think I should approach that problem?

What specifically do you need from me?

Here's the backup material that you requested this morning. Glad to be able to help.

I want to give you my complete attention so that I can fully understand the _____ (issue / directions / problem).

As I understand the issue, you need to focus on the Manning project today. How can I help you?

Are you saying _____? (Repeat back information as you understand it.)

Was this feedback helpful to you?

When I met with Ms. Simmons, she was concerned about the warranty. You might want to _____ (put her at ease about that / make her comfortable with that / explain that / outline it) first.

*I know it's late, but I haven't been able to get these numbers to match. Can you _____ (**give me a hand** / **lend me a hand** / **pitch in** / **take a shot at** this)?*

*Can we talk at 4 P.M.? I'm really _____ (busy / **tied up** / **in a bind**) now.*

*This customer needs help opening one of the bank's new checking accounts, and I think that you're _____ (**more up on that** / better at that / trained in opening these).*

*This deadline is really **closing in on** me. Could you possibly research this one area for me? It would be a **lifesaver**.*

*I'd be happy to **hand deliver** our team summary to the **VP**.*

*Hello, Mr. Wilkins. I'm Sally Lee from Auditing. I appreciated your remarks at the **kickoff** for our company **United Way** initiative.*

*I'm **all ears** for an hour, and then I have to leave for a meeting.*

Would you mind reviewing my meeting notes before I distribute them?

Phrases for Communicating with Colleagues/ Coworkers—Addressing Problems

*I regret that we _____ (**got off on the wrong foot** / **had a rocky start** / had that misunderstanding). Can we **get past it**?*

*I know how busy you are, but I have serious concerns about _____ (the **takeover** / our new direction / the results of this study / the report / my presentation). What would be a good time to talk about it?*

*Please find out what the **holdup** is. That way we can address the problem and speed things up.*

I am so sorry. I didn't realize that you had _____ (started on that account / talked to that customer before / begun the testing process on that drug / scheduled your presentation for that date). Of course _____ (that account / customer / drug test / presentation date) is yours.

Perfect Phrases to Keep Your Customers

Welcome to . . .

May I help you?

How can I help you?

I'll be with you in a minute; please have a seat.

Would you like a cup of coffee or a magazine while you wait?

I'm sorry to have kept you waiting.

Of course, Mrs. Lee, I can do that for you.

Thank you. I hope to see you again soon.

Please, let me _____ (hang that up for you / put that back on the shelf / get that information for you / show you a company brochure while you wait / introduce you to my counterpart who will help you while I'm gone).

You're welcome.

I'm so glad that I could help you.

Here's my card. Please call me with any questions.

Is there anything else I can do for you?

*I'd love to talk more, but I see another customer entering the store. Let's talk **in a bit**.*

How did the last game you bought work out? Did your grandchildren enjoy it?

Would you like that information sent by regular mail, fax, or e-mail? We'll do whatever is best for you.

You seem to have gotten off the elevator on the wrong floor. Michael Starr's office is on 11.

*Accounting is on the other side of the **atrium**. Please follow me, I'll take you there.*

I'm not sure. Let me call my supervisor—I don't want to give you incorrect information.

Did you know that we're having a sale starting Tuesday? Do you want me to hold _____ (that / that item)?

Perfect Phrases to Keep Your Customers— Addressing Problems

Please tell me what went wrong with that transaction.

I can see that you're upset. Let's review what happened and determine what I can do.

*To summarize: You called our offices with a direct request. Unfortunately, you don't recall the name of the representative who helped you. The transaction that you requested never occurred. Let me do a _____ (new / **fresh** / corrected) one _____ (and I can eliminate all fees / at no charge).*

Clearly you're angry. Let's go into the conference room so we can discuss this privately and find a solution that's satisfactory for you.

*Would you like me to call the **courtesy van**?*

Please let me know if you don't receive the reports that you requested by Friday.

Phrases for Communicating with Your Boss

*That's a strong suggestion. **I'll get right on it.***

Not a problem. I can have that to you by the end of today.

Can you take a minute to explain how you want this done?

I'll take notes so I don't have to ask again.

Okay. You want this to follow last year's report model, and you need it by next week.

I'm sorry, I didn't hear whether you wanted me to schedule a full team meeting or just the leadership team.

*I would love to **take the lead** on our departmental reporting process. Thank you for asking me.*

Judy, we can easily reformat that.

Tools for Improving Communication

The phrases in this chapter will help you improve your workplace communication, but also consider adding a good American English dictionary, a simple thesaurus, and a notebook and pen to your communication tool kit (which, of course, includes this book!).

A good and simple English or American English dictionary, preferably one with a CD (for audio pronunciation of entries) included, is a necessity. When you are new to the language, a bilingual dictionary works well for finding the words you need. However, as you progress in the language-learning process, direct translations don't always work, and it takes extra time to try to make a translation fit. American

English is loaded with idioms that don't translate directly to other languages. For example, consider the following:

Idiom	Meaning
It's raining cats and dogs	It's raining very hard
Don't let the cat out of the bag	Don't tell the secret or spoil the surprise
Pay through the nose	Pay a lot of money, too much money
Feel like a million dollars	Feel really terrific
Look like a million dollars	Look your best
Hot under the collar	Irate, extremely angry

Also, advanced American English dictionaries are **chock-full** of other valuable information—grammar rules, photos, drawings, information on American culture, and pronunciation.

Another essential language tool is a simple thesaurus. A thesaurus is different from a dictionary in that it directs attention to synonyms (words with the same meaning) and antonyms (opposites), not definitions, meanings, and pronunciation. For example, if you are writing or speaking about a meeting and repeating the word *meeting* over and over, it becomes very **repetitious**. If you look up *meeting* in your thesaurus, you will find synonyms that suit your need: *presentation, gathering, session, conference, convention*, and others. Like the dictionary, the thesaurus will also give you the part of speech, in this case noun.

You can find very large dictionaries and thesauruses (or thesauri) to keep at home or at the office, but the most useful ones for business communication are the smaller ones—not the pocket-size editions, but basic ones about five inches wide and eight inches long that fit in a briefcase.

A small notebook or pad and a pen that you can keep in your purse or pocket at all times are necessary tools. You may wish to write down anything you see, read, or hear and don't understand or anything you have trouble pronouncing to look up or ask an English-speaking friend about later. Include any questions you have so you can return to them and get them answered at a convenient time.

These are three very basic and indispensable tools. There are also valuable technological tools you may wish to investigate such as smart phone apps and ESL podcasts.

Idioms and Other Vocabulary

All ears: listening with undivided attention

(The) American way: something typically true of the American culture or an example of a usual behavior

Atrium: large, high open space in a building, often near the entryway

Chock-full: contains many/a lot

Closing in on: getting nearer to in either space or time

Consistent: always follows the same rule

Courtesy van: van sent by a hotel, car rental agency, automobile service center, or other site to take people to a location such as an airport, the site itself, or their home

Courtyard: open space surrounded by buildings or walls

Effective: producing the intended results

Fresh: new

Get past it: go on and pick up our relationship as it was before the misunderstanding

Give me a hand: help me

Glance: look quickly

Got off on the wrong foot: had a bad start to a relationship with a misunderstanding or an argument

Had a rocky start: had a bad start to a relationship with a misunderstanding or an argument

Hand deliver: give to someone by hand; physically hand to someone

Holdup: delay

I'll get right on it: I'll do it immediately

In a bind: in a difficult situation

In a bit: in a very short time

Justice of the peace: an official who performs marriage ceremonies

Kickoff: start or beginning

Left to chance: not planned

Lend me a hand: help me

Lifesaver: something or someone that saves one from a very difficult situation

Maid of honor: an unmarried woman who attends the bride in a wedding ceremony; a married woman who does this is called a matron of honor

Mother-in-law: one's spouse's (wife's or husband's) mother

Out of the blue: suddenly

Pitch in: help

Position yourself: put yourself in a good spot or place to achieve something

Preside: to be in charge of

Punch line: the end or the point of a joke

Repetition: saying or doing something again

Repetitious: said or done repeatedly

Run it by: check it out with

Sense of humor: ability to make people laugh and to understand humor

Take a shot at: try

Take the lead: go first

Takeover: act of getting control of a company by buying most of the stock in it

Tied up: busy

Till: short for until

United Way: a charity

Up on that: know about something

VP: vice president

Culture Hints: A sense of humor is a good thing to have in the American working world. Understanding what is considered funny in another culture is very difficult. It takes time and being sensitive to that culture. For example, **mother-in-law** and lawyer jokes are common in the United States. This doesn't mean that nobody gets along with his or her mother-in-law and that there are no good, honest lawyers. It does mean that those jokes are so common in the United States that even mothers-in-law and lawyers laugh at them. Don't start your presentation with a joke unless or until you **run it by** an American colleague or friend. There is nothing more painful than telling a joke and, after the **punch line**, hearing silence.

When speaking about a department in a company, you don't always say the full department title. You can say Auditing instead of the Auditing Department or HR instead of the Human Resources Department.

Many companies support charities, both local and national, by holding fund-raising events such as dinners, auctions, walk-athons or runs, and other initiatives to collect contributions.

Grammar Notes: Compound words form plurals by adding "s" to the main word. Examples include all in-law words. In-laws are related to you by marriage. Your mother-in-law is your wife's or husband's mother. If you have been married more than once, you could have had several mothers-in-law. When one has a formal wedding ceremony, the bride may have a **maid of honor**, or she may choose two maids of honor. One **justice of the peace** may **preside** over the ceremony, or two justices of the peace may share the honor. At work, there may be several managers-in-training. At least the rule is **consistent**.

Chapter 5

Dealing with Conflicts

Conflicts may arise in any situation in which you have more than one person: among family, friends, relatives, neighbors, acquaintances, people at a public place (a gym, a park, a disco), or at work. Conflict results from differences of opinion or **perception**. It may be caused by different personalities having to deal with a difficult situation. Often, different cultures handle disagreements in different ways; sometimes men and women have contrasting ways of acting in conflicting situations; labor and management have been known to have long-standing disagreements; and around November in the United States (election time), you may observe many conflicting political views.

Acknowledge that conflict will occur. Don't be **thrown by** it. Know how to **defuse** it, minimize it, even turn it into a friendly exchange or, on occasion, something to look back at and perhaps laugh at.

Conflict may also arise within an individual about difficult decisions or choices. We all have inner dialogues with ourselves. Sometimes these prepare us for the conflicting situations with others, and sometimes they get resolved and never make it outside our heads.

Phrases for Conflicts with Your Employer

I'm sorry; I should have asked for clarification before doing that. How can I correct that?

I'm sorry: I _____ (misunderstood / didn't hear you). How can I fix this?

I must have written down the wrong _____ (time / telephone number / area code / name / cross street). That won't happen again.

I realize that you are _____ (upset / angry / disappointed). Can we please talk about this in your office?

I'm sure that I put that _____ (letter / memo / contract) on your desk earlier, but here's another copy.

Thank you for agreeing to approach the problem the way that I suggested.

It was my understanding that you wanted the _____ (data / agenda / roster) next week. Am I right?

I would love to drop everything to do what you're asking. Is it okay if _____ (the filing / the budget / the documentation / the incident report) doesn't get done until tomorrow?

I know how important the _____ (dinner meeting / company picnic / awards ceremony) is, but I can't be there because my parents are arriving from India tonight.

Phases for Conflicts with Coworkers

Let's try to work out our schedules so we're both comfortable.

Let's work out a plan that will satisfy all key players.

Thank you for completing that _____ (transaction / sale / budget); I didn't realize that my meeting would last so long.

Although I prefer the early shift, I understand your pressures. Why don't you take the early time this week? No problem.

Please excuse me. I'd love to continue this conversation, but I have a deadline to meet.

By promising _____ (delivery / installation / repair) in two days, you created a _____ (difficult / impossible / frustrating) situation for our department.

*I appreciate that you have a major photocopying job. I only need to copy four pages for a 2 P.M. meeting. Do you mind if I _____ (interrupt / **cut in** / take a quick turn)?*

I have to get back to my desk, and I only need milk for coffee. Let me just sneak by you, please. This cafeteria is very crowded.

Phrases for Conflicts with Those Who Report to You

Please don't take my comments personally. I want you to _____ (succeed / make it / get the promotion / learn this system), and I hope this advice helps.

Please don't _____ (raise your voice / scream at me). I want to work this out, but we can't unless we can talk about it calmly.

We'll both look bad if the project isn't completed _____ (within the deadline / on budget / as agreed to).

*I would like to discuss this before one of us **blows this out of proportion**.*

Here's what I can do.

*I understand why you want to _____ (extend the deadline / ask for overtime), but how does that **impact** the team?*

34

How do you think you might have handled that customer interaction better?

I understand that you prefer that format, but my signature will be on the document and this is the way that I prefer it.

*I realize that you cannot get to work at 9 A.M. We have **flextime** options. Let's discuss this.*

Let's develop a schedule so that everyone doesn't take a lunch break at the same time.

*Our budget can no longer provide for the overtime that we've had in the past. This is **beyond my control**.*

Yes, all of our children's sports are important, but we can't let everyone out for every event.

Phrases for Conflicts Within Yourself

How do I feel about this?

I feel so conflicted. I don't know what to do.

Should I ask for _____ (a raise / a promotion)?

*I've been here for six months already. Am I **pulling my weight**?*

Do I have to wait for the performance evaluation, or may I ask my supervisor _____ (how I'm doing / for a raise)?

*What is my _____ (long-term goal / short-term objective / responsibility or **liability**) in this situation?*

What will I gain or lose by _____ (staying in this job / looking for another job / opening my own business)?

Will _____ (coming in earlier / working overtime / requesting training) help me reach my goal?

Will doing this hurt another person?

Idioms and Other Vocabulary

Beyond my control: outside of my power to do something about

Blow out of proportion: treat as larger and more important than it is

Cut in: get ahead of another person in line

Defuse: make a difficult, angry situation better

Enforced: strictly followed as set by law or agreement

Flextime: a work system that allows employees to work a specific number of hours with schedules that allow start and finish times convenient for them

Impact: have an effect on

Liability: legal responsibility

Perception: how one views (thinks about) a situation

Pulling my weight: doing my share of the work, doing what and how much I am supposed to do at work

Retire: stop working after having worked, usually at or after age 65

Thrown by: surprised by

Culture Hint: *These days, it is normal in the United States to think about career change and job change. Many people work at something for years and then decide they would like to make a change. Some even return to school either online, in evening classes, or full time (if they can afford it) in order to change careers. Additionally, many people take on new challenges after they **retire**. Some fields, usually physically demanding ones such as professional sports or fire or police personnel, have an **enforced** retirement deadline.*

Part 1 Notes Section

_____

_____

_____

_____

_____

_____

_____

_____

_____

_____

_____

_____

_____

_____

Part 2

The Written Word

"Nothing Is Impossible, but Some Things Are Very, Very Difficult"

An executive came from Japan for six months of intensive language training in the United States. He spent much time on vocabulary, grammar, listening, writing and spelling, and intercultural issues. He spent most of his learning time on pronunciation, especially the distinction between the sounds for the letters *L* and *R*, which is a major issue for many Japanese—and other Asians—learning to pronounce English.

This man was a wonderful student and an interesting and caring person. He worked very hard with three or four different trainers, and we all were sorry to see him leave and return to Japan. We had a farewell luncheon for him, and he said that he would **keep in touch** with us. He very quickly did just that. He wrote to thank us for all our help and our sincere friendship. He said that he showed his wife and children everything he studied and that his children loved learning from him.

He told us that he had returned to a salary raise and a much higher position in his company, and he was excited—and nervous—about his promotion. He went on to say that he would be returning to the United States for a couple of weeks and he wanted to have some more language training because he knew that he had to "*blush* up on his English." He did just that—he returned and **brushed up** on his English.

Chapter 6

Checks, Applications, and Other Forms

The written word has become everyone's responsibility—and everyone's business. Most employees have computers and write their own e-mails, letters, memos, reports, and other documents. That means that everyone requires a good grasp of basic grammar, usage, and punctuation. Everybody also needs the tools and skills to edit and **proofread** his or her own work. In addition to writing letters, memos, reports, and other business documents, you need the skills to complete applications, fill out forms, and even make out checks.

Checks

It may seem that writing a check is too small an issue to address here. But, as someone who has addressed this issue with many trainees at all levels of language learning and in all areas of the work world, I know that the topic of how to write a check correctly is one that needs attention. Writing a check is something that must be done accurately or it can cause one a lot of confusion including late fees, incorrect records, missed opportunities, and lost funds.

A check should be made out in pen, not pencil, and in black or blue ink rather than with a colored pen. The check number is already printed on the check, so start with the date. In many countries, the date is written with the day first, then the month, and finally the year. In the United States, we write the month first, then the day, and finally the year. May 10, 2010, or 5/10/2010, or 5/10/10, or 05/10/10 is correct; 10 May 2010 or 10/05/2010 or 10/5/10 is not correct in the United States (these latter forms would be interpreted as October 5, 2010). The form that the date is written in is very important because the bank will not clear a check earlier than the date for which it is written.

Do not **postdate** a check because if the writer of the check **passes away** before the date shown on the check, the check is **invalid**. Checks are usually **valid** for six months from the date written. If you **misplace** a check and then find it seven months later, ask the bank and the person who wrote the check if it can still be **honored**.

Make sure of the name of the person or business to whom you are making out the check so that you spell it correctly. Remember that it is more difficult to **forge** cursive writing than printing. When there is a difference between the numerical entry and the word entry of the amount, the word entry is the official amount. The small box for the numbers allows for only the numbers—the dollar sign is already printed. Write the numerical amount in one of the following ways: $10.75, $10.75/xxx; or $10.75/100. Print close to the dollar sign so that no one can add a number between the dollar sign and the numbers you have written. Remember, in the United States a decimal point or dot is used between the dollars and the cents, not a comma.

The word *dollars* is already written following the line on which you write out the amount in words, so don't rewrite it; you have enough to write. The cents should be written as a fraction, without using the word *cents*. At the end of the fraction draw a line up to the word *dollars*. This prevents anyone from writing anything else in this space. So Ten and 75/100——————————(Dollars) or Ten and 75/xxx——————————(Dollars) is correct.

Your signature at the bottom of the check must be written and not printed. Also, there is usually a place for a memo or a note about the check in the bottom left corner of the check. "Gift to Mary," "books for accounting course," and "6/17/11 utility bill" are examples of memos on checks.

Make certain that you write enough information in the **check register** so that you are able to match the register with your bank statement at the end of the month. Write the check number, the date, the person or business to whom the check was written, the amount, and the purpose of the check in the register.

Phrases About Writing a Check

This is my first check in the United States.

To whom do I make out this check: your business or you personally?

Please spell that for me.

I'd rather not give you this check today; I'll get it to you by Monday. I know the funds will be clear by then.

I need an invoice number to put on this check.

Do you need to see my (license / passport) for this check?

May I pay you in cash? My checks haven't been printed yet.

Phrases to Say at a Bank

What is the minimum amount I must keep in this account?

Are these checks free?

What is the charge, if any, when I reorder checks?

Is there a charge for deposit slips?

I just deposited a check for $400; how long will it take to clear?

Do I get any interest on the balance in my savings or checking account?

This check is drawn on an out-of-country bank; how long will it take to clear?

Will you process my application for an account today?

*Do I need to fill out a separate form to obtain an **ATM** card?*

Please tell me about the bank's credit and debit cards.

I often need money orders. Can I get them here, or do I have to go to a post office?

What is the charge for money orders?

What about traveler's checks?

Will the teller be able to help me with this, or should I wait for an officer?

Tell me about online banking, please.

Is there a Web site on which I can check my banking transactions?

Is there an 800 number I can call to check my balance instead of coming into the bank?

May I have one of your business cards?

*What are this **branch**'s hours?*

Are you open late any evenings? I don't leave work until 5 P.M.

What holidays are you closed?

*I notice there is no **drive-through** here. Do any of your other branches have drive-throughs?*

Applications and Other Forms

There are applications to fill out for practically everything in the United States. These applications or written requests are used to apply for most bank offerings: opening a savings or checking account, applying for a loan or a line of credit, asking to open a safe deposit box, or purchasing a savings bond, **for starters**.

There are forms to fill out involving cars and other motor vehicles, health and medical care and insurance, Social Security, change of address, and other postal issues including getting a post office box. Applying for credit and debit cards may be added to the list as well as store credit cards.

Some general rules apply to filling out all forms and/or applications: Read everything first, and be certain that you understand everything before writing. Make sure that the form is applicable to you and what you want or need. Check to be certain that you are willing to enter into whatever agreement is stated on the form or application because it is an agreement and your signature on it may make it a legally binding contract. Carefully follow the directions on the form. These directions may include using pen, using black ink, using a number 2 pencil, printing your text, printing legibly, writing your last name (surname or family name) first, and **so forth**. Don't **skip** any questions or sections—complete the form or it may be returned to you for corrections.

Employment applications are different from other applications in that many employers prefer that you fill out the employment applications at the **point of contact**. Employers are interested in checking your English language skills, so they don't want you to take an application and have another person fill it out for you. However, bank, automobile loan, and other applications should be **open for further review**. A useful hint is to ask for extra forms so that you can practice on one before completing the final copy. If it isn't possible to take more than one form, make a photocopy yourself to practice on instead.

Look carefully at the fees involved with an application: they may be nonrefundable or refundable within a certain time frame only, there may be a requirement for payment by check only or by credit card only, or the stated fee may be only one of several payments rather than the total cost. Be sure you understand the agreement or contract and the total cost involved before you sign the application or pay any fees.

Phrases for Filling Out Forms and Applications

I'll need extra time to read and understand this. English is not my first language.

Could you please clarify these directions? I don't want to make a mistake.

Can you explain this question on the form?

Do I have to _____ (answer all the questions / fill in number 7 / finish the whole form)?

May I borrow a pen? I don't have a pen with me.

May I have two copies of the _____ (application / form), please?

May I take this home and bring it back tomorrow or mail or fax it to you? Since English isn't my native language, I _____ (want to / need to / have to / would like to) go over a few items with _____ (the HR department where I work / my lawyer / my supervisor).

I don't have the answer to this question. May I take this home and fill it in there?

Would you please make a photocopy of my finished application so that I can save it for my records?

Is this one complete payment, and does it include all charges?

Is my payment refundable, and within how many days?

Idioms and Other Vocabulary

ATM: abbreviation for automatic teller machine

Branch: a separate store, office, or site of a large company, store, or bank in a different area

Brushed up: practiced or re-studied something already studied or learned

Check register: written record of check information including the date, check number, person or business to whom the check is written, amount, and purpose of the check

Downsized: fired for the purpose of reducing the size of a business

Drive-through: designed to allow customers to do business without getting out of their cars, such as a bank ATM or teller at a window; also used for fast-food restaurants, coffee shops, pharmacies, and other businesses

Euphemism: softer, more indirect words used in place of more direct words in order to be less dramatic or more polite

Fired: removed from one's job

Forge: copy something illegally, usually a signature

For starters: a beginning, there is more to follow

Honored: cashed, deposited, or accepted by the bank

Invalid: not true, real, or legal

Keep in touch: keep in contact

Let go: fired

Misplace: lose, put somewhere and not remember where

Open for further review: allowed to be taken with you to look at more carefully

Passes away: dies

Point of contact: the time that you meet a person, discuss an issue, and/or pick up an application

Postdate: to date later than the date you are actually writing the document

Proofread: to read and check written material for errors

Skip: leave out or omit

So forth: more of the same to follow

Terminated: fired

Valid: true, real, or legal

Culture Hint: *Americans, like people of many cultures, like to avoid harsh or unpleasant words, so we may substitute nicer, more indirect words or expressions called **euphemisms**. For example, instead of saying a person has died, we may say he or she* passed away, passed on, *or is* gone. *A number of euphemisms are used rather than saying that a person is **fired** from a job. People and companies use the more indirect terms **let go**, **terminated**, or **downsized** instead.*

Chapter 7

Faxes and E-mails

For most business writing, you have a number of delivery choices—e-mail, fax, postal service, or express delivery service. Both internal and external memos are primarily sent by e-mail. Faxes are still used, but far less frequently now than prior to the tremendous increase in the use of the Internet.

Faxes may be used if a signature is required on a document, if someone doesn't have the use of e-mail, or if the item being faxed is not on one's computer. Formal documents may be sent by e-mail for **expediency**, but are typically followed with **hard-copy** mailings.

E-mails can cut down on time and work. Not only are e-mails fast to send, but they can easily be forwarded or copied to other parties. They are perfect for quick and simple communication: checking on availability, offering congratulations, determining deadlines, seeking short answers to questions, etc. Remember, though, that you have to be careful in writing an e-mail. Documents on computers are easily accessed. Don't use your computer for personal e-mails or messages at work. Many companies monitor their employees' activities on their computers. Imagine that anything that you type on your computer can be read by anybody; think before you write.

Some written communications, especially thank-you notes, are best handwritten, stamped, and mailed. This last choice is now referred to as **snail mail**.

Whatever method you choose for sending your message, your grammar, usage, and spelling must be correct. Your writing is an extension of your image. When sending e-mail, put it in the "draft" folder and don't include an e-mail address initially, so that there is no chance of sending the e-mail before you have fully checked spelling, grammar, and meaning. You should have a spell-checker and grammar-checker on your computer, but that doesn't solve your problem entirely. For example, if you want to e-mail someone that there will be a short "wait" for the final project and you mistakenly type "weight," a spell-checker will not correct this because there is a word "weight" even though it isn't the correct one **in this case**. There are many examples of these **homophones**, or words that sound alike but have different meanings. **Homonyms** are also an issue, but a little different. (See the "Grammar Notes" sidebar at the end of this chapter.)

As far as a grammar check is concerned, that may also be **tricky**. Something may be corrected, and if you don't know why, you won't be able to correct the remainder of the writing **in context**. Again, you may check with an American colleague, but just as you may not know all of the grammar and spelling of your language, everyone educated in the U.S.A. doesn't know all the spelling and grammar of this country.

Perfect Phrases for Sending Faxes and E-mails

This is a very long printed form so I think I'd better fax it. What is your fax number?

I can fax you the proposal so you can review it and also see who signed off on it.

I will fax you my receipts from the Denver conference.

Just a quick note to let you know that . . .

Just checking in to see where you are with the monthly report.

Attached is a copy of the signed contract.

Congratulations on your _____ (promotion / award / daughter's marriage).

*Thanks for the _____ (**leg up** / update / kind words).*

I'm sending out _____ (the meeting minutes / a list of those requesting new lines of credit / the production schedule / revised vacation schedules). What is your e-mail address?

Please review and edit the attached _____ (letter / report / proposal / appropriation request).

*Please review the attached **draft** of the _____ (budget / proposal / newsletter). I'd like your comments and suggestions.*

*Please complete the attached application for the _____ (ESL course / German program / **Toastmasters** group / lunch and learn program).*

*Return the application to me as soon as possible so we can _____ (complete / **firm up** / organize) groups.*

*Hi—My schedule is _____ (**crazy** / **nuts** / **overwhelming**) next week. When are you free to discuss _____ (our **joint project** / the changes to our proposal / the new credit guidelines)? I'll try to _____ (**clear my calendar** / make time / change some things around / **fit you in**).*

*Please delete me from your **blast e-mail list**. I just don't have the time for so much e-mail that is not work-related.*

*The next meeting of _____ (the Chamber of Commerce / the finance committee / the Board / our team / the Union representatives) will be _____ (next Wednesday / December 1, at 9:30 A.M. / during lunch tomorrow). Please **RSVP ASAP** by e-mail.*

*Please send me your correct _____ (phone number / extension / schedule / badge number / code number) so I can ____ (complete the meeting **roster** / add it to the list I'm e-mailing to everyone / make the correct changes).*

Idioms and Other Vocabulary

ASAP: abbreviation for as soon as possible, each letter is usually said separately; sometimes, someone will pronounce it as a word, "a-sap"

Blast e-mail list: an e-mail list of a large group of people to whom you send the same e-mail message at the same time

Clear my calendar: change appointments to accommodate this one

Crazy: having much too much to do

Draft: writing not in final form

Expediency: quick and easy handling

Firm up: make definite

Fit you in: make time for you

Hard copy: copy of materials printed on paper rather than just read on a computer

Homonyms: words that sound and are spelled the same but have different meanings, such as *bear* in the following sentence: The *bear* could not *bear* the pain.

Homophones: words that sound the same but have different spellings and meanings, such as *wait* and *weight*

In context: relating to the words around the writing, the situation in which it is used

In this case: in this instance

Joint project: project worked on by more than one person or department

Leg up: extra help, head start, boost

Nuts: another expression that means doing too much at one time

Overwhelming: an overwhelming schedule is one that has far too much in it

RSVP: Abbreviation for the French phrase *respondez s'il vous plait*, which means "please answer"; pronounced as separate initials when found on invitations

Roster: list of people

Snail mail: mail sent through the United States Postal Service (USPS)—a recent nickname for correspondence because now e-mail is faster and mail—like snails—moves very slowly!

Toastmasters: an international public speaking group devoted to helping people improve their public speaking skills

Tricky: not straightforward, complicated

Culture Hint: *In the United States and other developed countries, technology moves very quickly. As someone once said, "With the invention of the airplane, we lost the wonder of the birds." So it is a balancing act and you have to develop a "feel" or sensitivity for what is appreciated more in each separate situation. For example, if it is a colleague's birthday, you may just say, "Happy Birthday," send an e-mail card, send a card through the mail, put a card on his or her desk, have lunch with him or her, or any number of other things. This would depend on the culture of the company in which you work, your feelings about birthdays in general and your colleague in particular, and what you know about your colleague's feelings about birthdays in general and you. There's where sensitivity comes in and it is always subjective. Don't worry, in this case you aren't going to make a major mistake.*

Grammar Notes: Homophones are words that sound the same as other words, but have different spellings and meanings, such as wait *and* weight. *Other homophones you may use:*

To: *part of an infinitive verb such as* to write; *in the direction of*
Two: *the number 2*
Too: *also, over the limit*

Cite: *to quote*
Sight: *to have vision*
Site: *location*

Know: *be acquainted with*
No: *opposite of* yes

There: *at that place; not here*
Their: *belonging to them*
They're: *contraction for "they are"*

Hole: *an opening or empty space through or in something*
Whole: *entire, all*

Knew: *past tense of* know
New: *opposite of* old

Hear: *to listen*
Here: *in this location*

Weak: *not strong*
Week: *seven days*

By: *close or near; no later than*
Buy: *purchase*

Homonyms are words that sound the same and are spelled the same, but have different meanings, such as two of the meanings of bow: *a long stick used to play a stringed musical instrument and a tied ribbon on a gift or a tied end of a shoelace. Both are spelled "bow" and both are pronounced /bo/.*

Chapter 8

Memos, Notes, and Letters

E-mails and faxes are methods for sending written information. Memos, notes, and letters are different kinds of written information. All can be sent by e-mail, fax, or regular mail. For memos, quick notes, and even many letters, e-mail has become the method of choice. Mailing a handwritten note still **earns points** when a more personal means of communicating is valued by the **recipient**. People appreciate the extra effort. Certain letters, especially those with legal **ramifications** or those that contain **confidential** information, should be mailed.

Memos are typically for internal communication. However, whether you are sending memos within your company or to those outside of it—clients, customers, **vendors**, and others—you are probably sending them by e-mail. Notes may be sent by e-mail, but they are often handwritten and mailed. Letters, too, may go the e-mail route. It is faster, easier to track, and usually gets a faster response.

Memos usually begin with "To:" and "From:" lines (or the "From:" line may be first). Now that so many memos are written as less-formal e-mails, many begin with "**FYI**" (which means "for your information") and include a salutation such as "Hi, (first name)," "Hi," "Hello, (first name)," "Hello," "Hello, Everyone," "Dear (first name)," "Dear (Mr. / Ms. / Mrs. / Dr.) (last name)," or "Dear (Staff / Committee Members /Team)." E-mails often include a "subject line" that tells what they are about, such as "Monday's staff meeting" or "Questions on Wilson account."

Perfect Phrases for Sending Memos

The Monday morning _____ (meeting / class / workshop / session / program) has been canceled. Please forward this memo to everyone in your department immediately.

Please review the **tentative** agenda below and send a short response to confirm that you are in agreement.

I'm forwarding Mike's e-mail about the **security breach**. The points that he makes are **critical**; please share with your _____ (department / staff / team / group).

I _____ (apologize / am sorry / must be **losing it** / have looked everywhere / **searched high and low**) and I cannot _____ (locate / find / **retrieve**) the schedule that you sent to me. Could you please e-mail another?

The attached **draft** report is due to Corporate by Thursday. Please _____ (review / look it over / proofread / edit / check it out) and return with your comments.

All staff must read, **initial**, and return this memo describing changes in our medical coverage. Please _____ (circulate / **route** / distribute) one copy for all signatures.

Perfect Phrases for Sending Notes

Thank you for the delicious lunch; it was _____ (informative / helpful / interesting) meeting with you. I _____ (learned a lot / appreciate your time / hope we can do it again).

Just a note to let you know how much I appreciated your help.

I wanted to let you know how _____ (**on target** / well done) your recent presentation was. Keep up the good work.

Welcome to the company. Please let me know if you need anything.

Perfect Phrases for Letters

*The enclosed contracts are signed by our representatives. Please have your _____ (**reps** / representative(s) / officer / manager / supervisor / director of production) sign and return them.*

Thank you for taking time to learn about _____ (our product / our service). I will call you next week to answer any questions you might have.

*Please review the _____ (enclosed / attached) _____ (brochure / **pamphlet** / description / **endorsement**). I look forward to meeting with you to share more detailed information.*

*Thank you for letting us know about your dissatisfaction with our _____ (product / service / actions / lack of response). We regret that our _____ (name item or service) didn't meet your needs. Please accept the enclosed _____ (refund check / coupons / products / check). We hope we can **exceed expectations** in the future.*

*Thank you for **commending** the _____ (service / work) of _____ (name of employee). We are very pleased with the pride that he takes in his work and our products. Customers are always his first priority, and _____ (name of company) is very _____ (proud of / happy with) him. (Substitute she/her as appropriate.)*

This letter confirms that _____ (name), our _____ (manager / supervisor) of _____ (quality control / production / sales / service) will address the _____ (Trade Conference / Union Meeting / Annual Session) on behalf of _____ (name of company) on January 16, 2011, in Chicago.

Phrases for Opening Letters

Dear _____ (first name),

Dear _____ (Mr. / Ms. / Mrs. / Dr.) _____ (last name),

Dear _____ (Staff / Committee Members / Team),

Phrases for Closing Letters

Sincerely,	*With Appreciation,*
Sincerely yours,	*Thanks,*
Cordially,	*Thank you so much,*
Yours truly,	*Regards,*
Very truly yours,	*Best regards,*

Idioms and Other Vocabulary

Commending: saying/writing nice words about

Confidential: private, secret

Critical: extremely important

Draft: written material not in final form

Earn points: get extra recognition

Endorsement: approval

Esquire or Esq.: title of respect, only after names of lawyers

Exceed expectations: achieve more than or beyond what one is expected to

First name: given name, the name your parents gave to you

Full name: your entire name

FYI: acronym for "for your information"; used at the top of internal and external memos; each letter is pronounced separately

Given name: the name your parents gave to you

Initial: to write the first letters of one's name on something—for example, *JHS* for John Harry Smith

Last name: your family name or surname

Losing it: losing control of oneself

Maiden name: a woman's last name before marriage

Middle name: a second given name that is usually used less often if at all

Nickname: shorter form of one's given name, or a descriptive name used by family or friends (for example, the nickname for Nicholas might be Nico, Nicky, or Nick, but it might also be "Music Man" because Nicholas loves music)

On target: correct, to the point, addressing the issue

Pamphlet: informative papers thinner than a book, but in booklet form

Ramifications: consequences

Recipient: person, business, or charity that receives something

Rep: short term for representative

Retains: keeps

Retrieve: get back

Route: circulate one copy among many people instead of giving a copy to each person

Searched high and low: looked all over

Security breach: broken rule of safety

Surname: a formal way to say last name or family name

Tentative: uncertain

Title: prefix to name that indicates gender and/or marital status, academic degree, occupation, or an honorary appellation, such as *Mr.*, *Mrs.*, *Miss*, *Ms.*, *Dr.*, *President*, etc.

Vendors: outside companies used to provide services or products to your company, for example food and catering services, maintenance, or promotional items

Culture Hints: *In the United States, there are many words associated with names. John Fitzgerald Kennedy, the 35th president of the United States, is a good example with which to study this. His **first name** or **given name** was John; his **nickname** was Jack; his **middle name**, which was his mother, Rose Fitzgerald Kennedy's, **maiden name**, was Fitzgerald; and his **surname** or **last name** was Kennedy, his father Joseph P. Kennedy's last name. Therefore, this President's **full name** was John Fitzgerald Kennedy.*

*His **title** was President, and a President **retains** that title always, even when there are many presidents after him, so we call him President John F. Kennedy or President Kennedy.*

Other nicknames for the first name John are Johnny, Johnnie, and Jackie, to name a few (though these were not President Kennedy's nicknames as far as we know). People may have one or more middle names, may use their mother's family name as a middle name, or may only use an initial, as President Kennedy's father, Joseph P. Kennedy, did.

*When addressing someone formally or addressing an envelope to someone, you would want to use a title. Familiar ones include Mr. (pronounced "Mister"), Mrs. ("Missus," a married woman), Miss, an unmarried woman, and Ms. (from a blend of Miss and Mrs., pronounced "Miz"), marital status unknown. There are also titles such as Dr. (Doctor) for those with advanced degrees like M.D. or Doctor of Medicine; D.D.S., Doctor of Dentistry; Ph.D., Doctor of Philosophy; Psy.D., Doctor of Psychology; Ed.D., Doctor of Education; or L.L.D., Doctor of Law. The name of a medical doctor, Mary Brown, could be written as "Dr. Mary Brown" or "Mary Brown, M.D." Lawyers often use **esquire (Esq.)** after their names.*

Chapter 9

Larger Writing Projects

At times, you may be asked to write something beyond a letter or a memo. Depending on your job, you may have to write a **job description**, a **credit request**, an **appropriation request**, an **incident report**, a **project proposal**, or any of a number of longer writing projects. The person requesting the project may give you very clear direction. On the other hand, many people do not give clear direction. They may not be sure of what they want until they see it, or worse, until they see what they don't want. They may assume that you have a **mirror image** in your head of what's in theirs, or they may think that they've been clear.

The best way to save time for both yourself and the person who asks you to write something is to get clarification **up front** and, if possible, have the person review your drafts along the way. The larger the project, the more information you want to have before you begin. You don't want to spend hours or days writing something that does not meet the requirements. If you are the one assigning the writing project, **take** this advice **to heart** and be sure to give clear direction.

Phrases for Getting Clarification for a Writing Project

*Do you want to see an outline before I **flesh out** the strategic plan?*

*Gerry and I are working on the _____ (**request for proposal** / strategic plan / **ad script** / **bulletin**) together. Do you want to give us direction before we begin?*

To save us both editing time, please let me know _____ (some key points / your favorite phrase for positive news / the core message) and anything else I should know about your writing style before I begin the draft.

*I prefer to **jump into** a draft without outlining. Once I get my thoughts down on paper and review them, I can go back and create an outline for you. Will that work?*

*Do you have a copy of a recent _____ (proposal / request / document / **brochure** / pamphlet) that met with your approval so that I can model mine after it?*

How many _____ (pages / words / copies) do you want?

This completed document is due a week from Thursday. May I show you an outline later today and a draft on Monday? That should keep this on track and moving in the right direction.

Please check my _____ (grammar / vocabulary / punctuation). In some contexts, I was not sure of _____ (the correct verb form / the right word).

Phrases for Giving Clarification for a Writing Project

Before you start, please review this file of previous, similar documents.

*I know how hard it is for some people to change course once they start writing. Please give me a _____ (detailed outline / summary / plan / **step-by-step** process) to review before you invest a lot of time on the draft.*

*I like to review an outline first, then a draft. By the time we've **dissected** those, the final writing is usually a **piece of cake**.*

This _____ (proposal / funding request / presentation outline) is going to the Board of Directors. Please don't write informally. Choose your words carefully.

For those who work with me on _____ (proposals / projects / presentations), I recommend having copies of Strunk and White's The Elements of Style *and* The Gregg Reference Manual ***handy*** *for reference.*

Since several of you are writing _____ (capital appropriations requests / credit requests / sales proposals), I've scheduled a brief seminar to review the format and key elements. Please bring any _____ (grammar / usage / vocabulary / punctuation) questions you have as well.

Before you hand the final draft in to me, please let Josie review it. She's a great editor.

*When you edit one another's work, please don't use a green pen. That's our CEO's **signature** editing tool. Consider it **proprietary**.*

*Once our requests have been approved or denied by the **powers that be**, we will have a **Monday morning quarterback** session to determine how we can improve the next round.*

Idioms and Other Vocabulary

Ad script: *ad* is short for advertisement; a *script* is the written form of what is to be said

Appropriation request: a request for money (usually a large amount) from a department in a company to the finance committee or department. For example, engineering departments often submit capital appropriation requests (CARs) to a CAR committee for approval.

Brochure: a printed piece that describes a company, product, or service

Bulletin: a printed paper that offers news

Credit request: A banking term—a loan officer submits a credit request to the loan department of a commercial bank on behalf of the client; the credit request must be approved before a loan is issued

Dissect: take apart, pick apart, carefully review (from the scientific process of surgically taking apart a dead animal to examine its internal structure)

Divvied up: divided among several people

Flesh out: Fill out completely; add more information to an outline, a general idea, or plans for a project

Handy: available and useful

Incident report: An official report about something that happens in the workplace such as a confrontation between two employees or an employee and a customer, an accident, or a problem such as a pipe bursting or security equipment not working properly

Job description: a description of the specific roles and responsibilities of a particular job and the knowledge, skills, and experience required to do it well

Jump into: get immediately involved, begin instantly

Mirror image: an exact image as seen in a mirror

Monday morning quarterback: looking back at a situation to see what went wrong and how it could have been handled better (This is a sports reference. Football games in the United States are typically played and shown on television on Sundays. On Monday morning, many who saw the game are convinced that they could have done a better job with strategy than the coach or quarterback for the losing team.)

Piece of cake: easy

Project proposal: a written description of how one would work on a specific project

Proprietary: belonging to someone, owned

Powers that be: those in charge, decision makers

Request for proposal (RFP): a formal document asking for proposals to complete a particular project

Signature: distinctive or characteristic (from the distinct way each person signs his or her name); for example, many chefs have signature dishes, and outstanding professional athletes have signature moves

Step-by-step: process divided into parts and in order of first to last acts performed

Take something to heart: take it seriously, believe it

Up front: at the outset, before you start

Culture Hint: *Often specialized consultants are called in or hired for large writing projects. However, if the company downsizes and cuts back on the use of consultants, such writing projects increasingly may be* **divvied up** *among the company regulars.*

Grammar Notes: Between *and* among *are used differently.* Between *refers to time or space that separates two people, things, groups, or ideas. For example,* "There is a difference between *the Democratic Party and the Republican Party in the United States." "Between* you and me, *I find it a difficult choice."* Among *refers to something being shared by three or more people, things, groups, or ideas. For example,* "There was not one doctor among *the passengers on the airplane, so the plane had to make an emergency landing. There was a surgeon* among *the people in the airport.* Among *the four of us, I was really glad that doctor was there."*

Chapter 10

Proofreading

Proofreading or proofing means rereading what someone has written in order to find and correct errors in spelling, grammar, and **usage**. The proofreading step is your final chance to catch errors. You are responsible for everything you have proofread and, certainly, for everything that has your signature. Remember the "Five C's": Check the copy completely, carefully, and correctly. Proofreading your own work is **essential**, but often it is not enough. Have at least one other person proofread what you've written. Remember that you cannot proofread your work—or someone else's—efficiently if you are rushing or **distracted**. Good proofreaders read **out loud**, if it's at all possible. It's amazing what you can catch when reading **aloud** that you might miss when reading silently.

Another tip is to **point to** each word. Also, use a **straightedge** to keep your place. That way, you won't **inadvertently** skim over words. A good "one, two, three, and four rule of proofreading" is:

1. Read first for sense. Reading forward is reading for meaning.
2. Read second for accuracy. Focus on correct word usage, e.g., suffixes, homophones, etc.
3. Read third, from right to left, to **scrutinize** each word. This reading backward step usually catches spelling errors.
4. Read, again, double checking numbers, dates against calendars, names, and unfamiliar information.

Proofreading is especially difficult for those for whom English (at least American English) is a second language. You may not know all the vocabulary; you certainly will not have **come across** most of the idioms; you will **have issues** with some of the spelling, even if it is simply the difference between British English and American English spelling; and there also may be unfamiliar information.

The grammar-checker and spell-checker functions of your word processing software are useful, but they need to be **monitored**. These are mechanical tools: as we discussed in chapter 7, they miss **nuances** such as an incorrect homonym or a word that doesn't make sense in the context but is spelled correctly. These tools may miss other errors as well.

Following are some of the more popular standard proofreading marks that you may find on your work when it has been read by others. Also, you may want to use these when you are proofreading material and passing it on to the next proofreader. A full list of proofreading symbols is readily found in usage references (such as *The Gregg Reference Manual* or *The Chicago Manual of Style*) or on the Internet.

(stet)...	Stet, keep something that was crossed out
	Delete, take out
(cap) ☰	Uppercase, use capital letters
(l.c.) /	Lowercase, use non-capital or "small" letters
∪	Close space, remove space between letters or words
#	Add space
∧	Insert
⊙	Insert period

//   Align

(tr) ∿   Transpose, switch places

(¶) ∠   New paragraph

Proofreading Phrases

Yes, I've completed the document, but I need to proofread it.

Please show me how to use the spell-checker program on my computer.

English isn't my first language. Would you please look this over for me?

I've used the spell-checker, read out loud, and read by pointing, but I'm still concerned that I may have missed something. Would you please read this over?

I often _____ (misspell Governor / use the wrong there / write good instead of well). Could you check this document for those errors in particular?

I've learned not to _____ (count on / rely on / trust) the spell-checker. I have to double check everything.

The spell-checker let this error go through. It is a word, but not the right word in this context.

I can't believe that this _____ (pamphlet / report / proposal / brochure) has errors. Three of us read it.

Would you like me to proof what you have written? The manager is a stickler for accuracy.

You can always use an extra pair of eyes.

Our company's policy of using two proofreaders for every external document is an excellent idea.

*We're printing 1,000 copies of these brochures on Monday. Please _____ (check the original carefully / catch even the smallest errors / **run** all the corrections **by** me) by noon.*

Would you please pass this to Maria to proof after you have read and corrected it? I need to send it out this week.

*I'd say this is correct **off the top of my head**, but let me proof it carefully before you _____ (print it / send it / forward it / scan it / show it to the boss / make many copies).*

Idioms and Other Vocabulary

Aloud / out load: spoken in a normal voice in order for you to hear yourself

Columnist: someone whose job it is to write regularly for a newspaper or other media outlet; originates from the fact that newspapers are printed in columns

Come across: to find or find out accidentally

Context: the surrounding words or information

Count on: trust

Distracted: thinking about other things, not focused

Essential: absolutely necessary

External document: written material sent outside of your company

Extra pair of eyes: another person to proofread, check, look for errors

Have issues: have problems

Inadvertently: without planning to do it

In particular: especially

Monitored: watched carefully

Nuances: slight differences or changes

Off the top of my head: just from looking at something quickly, not studying it

Point to: indicate with your finger

Proof: proofread
Rely on: trust
Run by: let have a look at
Scrutinize: look at or read very carefully
Stickler for: cares about more than is necessary or usual
Straightedge: ruler
Strictly speaking: stated in a rigid or exact way
Usage: how words and phrases are correctly used
Well taken: accepted as valid or helpful

Culture Hint: *My favorite example of incorrect **usage** occurred many years ago. Then–New York City mayor John Lindsay sent a memo to the popular newspaper **columnist** Art Buchwald. At the top of Mayor Lindsay's memo paper was printed "From the Desk of John Lindsay, Mayor of New York." Art Buchwald replied to the memo with the opening, "Dear Desk." He was joking, of course, but his point is **well taken**. Mayor Lindsay's printed words were correct, but used badly—**strictly speaking**, a desk cannot write!*

Part 2 Notes Section

Part 3

Moving Up

"A Drawing of Recommendation"

Many years ago, a colleague came to our office to work on a project with me. She had to bring her son, Jamie, with her, a troubled seven-year-old who wouldn't go to school that day or stay with a **sitter**. The boy was very **disturbed** about his parents' divorce.

A young man interning in our office, Drew, asked the boy to take a walk with him to a basketball court on the property and **shoot some hoops** so his mom could work more efficiently. Surprisingly, the boy agreed, and they left.

When the intern and the boy returned an hour and a half later, the boy seemed calmer and happier. Jamie thanked Drew and left with his mom. Later that week, Drew received an envelope with a drawing of a man and a boy playing basketball and a sweet, **hand-printed** thank-you note. Drew—and all of us—were very touched by this.

The next year, Drew applied to **grad school**; this was part of his **long-range plan**. He wanted to earn a doctorate in psychology. He used Jamie's drawing as one of his **letters of recommendation**. Drew was accepted to graduate school, and perhaps the picture had something to do with it. We're sure no one else sent in a "drawing of recommendation." It **fit the situation**, and that makes a difference, especially in a **competitive arena** such as applying to schools, competing in the job market, and other situations in which **standing out in a crowd** makes a difference in your chances to **come in first at the finish line**. Drew is now a child psychologist, and Jamie is happy and successfully running a restaurant.

Chapter 11

Networking for Stepping Up

You may be **moving on up** within your present company, **stepping up** to new opportunities and responsibilities in another setting, or possibly going **out on your own**. Whatever the plan is, you'll be networking, submitting résumés and letters of recommendation, participating in interviews, and following up in all of these areas. In some instances this will be different from what you did to get your first job in the United States, but in other cases it will be quite similar, **skill-wise**. Keep in mind that you've been there before, and this time your language skills are much improved.

Networking Within Your Own Organization

Networking within your own organization or company is not as easy as it initially sounds. Yes, you and the people you wish to work with are all there in one place, but you all have your own **niches**, work schedules, work habits, and **comfort zones**. Often, in large companies, people don't easily get to know people in other departments. Getting to know people beyond your limited **sphere** of work is important for many reasons. The more people you know, the more comfortable you will be in a variety of work situations. The broader your circle of working relationships, the more opportunities you have for growth, learning, and assistance. An added benefit for you is hearing more English, using more English, and connecting more with the work culture in the United States.

You may get to know people in the company cafeteria, seeing someone regularly in the elevator, attending interdepartmental meetings, or working on **cross-functional** projects. Take a vacant seat at a table in the cafeteria with a group of people you've never met. Say hello to someone you often see in the elevator. Offer to help out on interdivision get-togethers. Introduce yourself to the CEO in the hallway. Your work may have an effect on the productivity of someone you haven't met or **vice versa**.

Networking within your organization will not only help you with your current job but may open doors for future moves within the company. Also, none of your efforts will be wasted if you move outside of the company or out on your own.

Phrases for Networking Within Your Own Organization

Hi. Do you mind if I _____ (join you / sit here / take a seat)? I'm Vi Lam from the _____ (Service / Sales / Production / Advertising / Loan / Credit / HR) Department.

*Hello again. We seem to _____ (always take this elevator together / have the same schedule / meet in elevators). I'm Shu Chou, _____ (Mr. Hendrick's assistant / Jim Hendrick's **admin** in Accounting). And you are? _____ (Nice to meet you / Nice to put a name with a face / Good talking to you).*

*This is Rick from _____ (Facilities Management / Food and Beverage / Audiovisual / Support). I called because you have several meetings scheduled next month. I know there was a _____ (problem / **glitch** / difficult situation) with the setup last month. Can we get together to review your specific requirements? We _____ (**aim to please** / want things to work better / want to be **on the same wavelength**).*

*Charlie, are you going to the Department Awards Dinner? I've never been to one before and would appreciate walking in with a **friendly face**. Do you mind?*

*I'm glad to be a part of this cross-functional team. Our department has always felt a little _____ (isolated / set apart / **like a stepchild**). What can I do to **pull my weight**?*

*Thank you for getting that _____ (Incident Report / budget detail / requisition / credit report / **ISO 9000** quality standards page) in so quickly. It's hard to reach out across so many department lines. I appreciate working with you.*

*May I **shadow** you during the next round of meetings? It will help me better understand how to support you for the follow-up.*

*I heard that you are now on the Advisory Committee for **Going Green**. Is there anything I can do to help? The environment has always been of special interest to me.*

*May I present our capital appropriation request to the Board? I'd like to **get my feet wet**, and this one is pretty **cut-and-dried**.*

Forgive me, but I'm new to this group. Could we take a minute for introductions? I'd like to know everyone's name and department. Thanks for taking the time.

Hi. This is Jenny from Operations. A call to your department was misdirected to me. May I transfer Ms. Lang, who has a question about our renewal process?

Hi Gina, I'm Ellen. We've been talking on the phone quite a bit trying to solve that _____ (meeting arrangement / customer service problem / scheduling conflict between our bosses).

Oh, that was my pleasure!

(Excuse me, Ms. Lane. / You're Ms. Lane, aren't you? / I believe that you are Ms. Lane.) I'd like to introduce myself and tell you how much I enjoy working at _____. I'm Sonny Grier. I work with John Karlen in Accounting.

Networking Outside Your Own Organization

You may be content at your organization, with no thought of looking for a job elsewhere, but you can never predict when the economy, a merger, or a personality clash will make leaving a necessity. In bad economic times, or when a company is not performing, there may be **downsizing** or **cutting back**. Employees may be offered (or strongly encouraged to take) **buyout packages**. They then look to work in other companies or **go off on their own**. With these scenarios in mind, networking outside your own organization is quite simply a necessary career tool.

And remember, too, that if you offer to help others, they are usually eager to help you.

Phrases for Networking Outside of Your Company

Hi, my name is Mohammed Patel. I've just opened a _____ (consulting firm / insurance agency / lawn care business / fast-food franchise / day care center).

I'm Barbara Sims, new partner in Quik Copy printing.

_____ (Here's my / Thank you for taking my / I'd like to give you my) business card.

Can you recommend an industry conference that would be good to attend? I'd like to meet more people in my field.

I'm finding this convention useful—are you?

Would you mind if I sit next to you during this workshop? I'm _____ (your name) from Denver, Colorado.

Let me know if I can help you with your travel needs. I now work for Airport Limos.

What's your business? Perhaps I can refer people to you. I've been attending many meetings lately, and I meet a lot of new people.

You'll also find phrases for general networking and for networking outside your company in *Perfect Phrases for ESL: Everyday Business Life.*

Idioms and Other Vocabulary

Admin: short for administrative assistant

Aim to please: goal to perform well

Buyout package: advantages offered to employees to leave (such as cash payments, increased severance, etc.) when a company downsizes

Come in first at the finish line: win

Comfort zone: area or situation in which one feels comfortable

Competitive arena: a situation in which many people are trying to fill few openings

Consultant: someone with the knowledge of a particular area and advises in that area

Cross-functional: comprised of people from a number of different departments within a company

Cut-and-dried: well-planned, easy, not complicated

Cutting back: spending less

Disturbed: worried, upset

Downsizing: making less or smaller

Fit the situation: was appropriate for the occasion

Friendly face: someone you already know, recognize

Get my feet wet: try or do something for the first time

Glitch: small problem that stops something from working well

Going green: becoming environmentally aware, implementing practices that reduce waste, save energy, and/or encourage recycling

Go off on one's own: go into one's own business

Grad school: graduate school, university, or college where you can study for an advanced degree

Hand-printed: printed (not written) by hand, not created on a typewriter or word processor

ISO 9000: international standards that set up requirements for certification for manufacturers or service industries

Letters of recommendation: formal letters saying that someone is appropriate for the job

Like a stepchild: treated less favorably than others

Long-range plan: an intention of what you want to do for a time in the future

Moving on up: improving yourself at work and advancing in your career

Niche: particular slot that fits your skills and talents

On the same wavelength: having the same thought processes

Out on your own: in your own business, not with a company

Pull my weight: do something meaningful to show that I am a working member of the committee or team

Shadow: follow someone around at work and observe in order to learn

Shoot some hoops: play basketball

Sitter; also babysitter: a person who takes care of children while their parents aren't home

Skill-wise: in terms of the skills needed for the process

Small scale: as a hobby or part time

Sphere: area

Standing out in the crowd: being noticed because of being better than others in a group

Stepping up: improving yourself at work

Vice versa: the opposite order of what has just been expressed

Culture Hint: Small businesses, women-owned businesses, and entrepreneurs going into their own businesses have become common in the United States. Many people have started their own businesses on a **small scale** while still employed. This gives them an opportunity to go into this business after an early retirement from the company for which they work. For example, an art teacher in a school may start a calligraphy business preparing invitations and other artwork. A good pastry baker, who may have begun baking as a hobby, can develop a side business cooking pies and cakes, no matter what his or her other job is. Many people are also **consultants**. They give advice to others on their area of expertise, such as decorating, organizing, or nutritional counseling. For some specialties, you need a degree, for some a certificate, and for some only knowledge in the area.

Chapter 12

Job Applications, Résumés, and Cover Letters

For some jobs, you'll need to fill out an application. The application may be sent to you if you call about an advertised job, or you may be given one when you go in person to inquire about a position or report for an arranged interview. If the application is sent to you or you can pick it up and take it home, you may fill it out in the comfort of your home, school, or even a library. Often, though, you have to complete it **on-site** at the company without the benefit of a spell-checker or grammar-checker. Review the information about applications in general in Chapter 6 along with the following tips specific to job applications.

It's a good idea to come prepared with a personal information paper you have carefully written out beforehand that contains information you may be asked to write on an application. You will be able to use this information to fill out the application rather than having to start thinking about it for the first time with the application in front of you. In addition to your personal information paper, bring scrap paper to practice on, a few pens with black or blue ink, relevant documentation, and a small bilingual dictionary for quick, emergency translations.

Answer honestly all the questions that **pertain** to you and the job you are applying for. For questions that don't apply, write **N/A (not applicable)** or just a dash (—) in the space after the question to indicate that you have read and understood the question, but that question doesn't apply to you. For example, the question, "Do you have an electrician's license?" may be N/A to you if you are not applying for work that involves electrical knowledge or experience.

Phrases for Preparing Job Applications

_____ (Could you / Would you / Please can you) help me complete this application.

There are _____ (a few parts / some words / a couple of questions) on this application that I _____ (don't understand / need help with / think don't apply to me).

I'd like _____ (a duplicate / a second / another) copy, please. I like to fill out a practice one first.

Do I have to _____ (complete both sides / answer all 30 questions / complete this form here) before I _____ (speak with someone / find out more about the work / ask you some questions)?

I have only been in the United States for nine months, and the application asks for personal references who have known me for at least three years. What should I do?

I'm in the United States with my family, and the form wants references who are not relatives. I don't know other people here.

My diploma is in _____ (your language). _____ (Can someone translate it / Should I tell you what it says / Do you need me to come back with someone who is bilingual)?

83

Résumés

It's a good idea to have an updated résumé saved on your computer and a few copies in your files **at the ready** at all times. The first time you prepare a résumé in the United States will be the most difficult. After that, you will have a better idea of what employers are looking for. You can also rearrange parts of the résumé on your computer to suit the particular jobs you are applying for.

You have most likely heard the words **curriculum vitae (CV)** used interchangeably with résumé, but they are different. A CV is much longer than a résumé. It lists all the courses you have taken during your education as well as publications and other achievements since it is used almost exclusively when applying for academic or teaching positions at colleges and universities.

Résumés in many countries are long—four or five pages—and **created equal**. In other words, you would send the same résumé out for any job for which you are applying. Résumés in the United States are shorter, usually one to two pages. The résumé is a sales presentation to **sell you**. You must give adequate information, but also be concise. This becomes a **balancing act**. Also, **one size doesn't fit all**. You should rearrange the résumé to fit the position you are applying for by making the most important information related to that position stand out. A **cover letter** should accompany each résumé you send out. This letter should **delineate** special information about your qualifications related to the particular job.

There are two basic types of résumés, and the types may also be combined. A **chronological résumé** lists your work experience in date (year) order, starting with the most recent. A **functional résumé** focuses on your specific skills and experiences rather than the dates and companies where you worked.

The résumé format is **unique**. The object is to make the recipient want to read the résumé. Leave a lot of white space, making margins wider than usual. Use a white or light colored (beige, cream, gray) good quality paper. Single space within each section, but double space between sections. Center the text or justify left (align on the left margin but not on the right). Capitalize headings. Be **consistent** with form. There is much information on preparing résumés on the Internet and in book form with sample résumés. Also, it is wise to ask an American friend or colleague to look over your résumé. This is an important document, and you don't want the reader to whom you are sending it to notice any errors or put the résumé down before he or she finishes reading it.

Today, many companies and employment agencies request that prospective employees fax or e-mail their résumés. If you have a variety of résumés stored on your computer, carefully identify them. Always print the résumé before faxing or e-mailing it just to check that you are sending the correct version.

Phrases to Think About When Writing a Résumé

What is my work experience in the United States, in my country, in other countries?

Is my experience relevant to the position I am applying for?

Is my experience transferable?

Are my skills transferable to another type of job?

What are my qualifications?

*What do I want to present as my **objective**?*

What specific skills should I highlight?

*Do I have particular accomplishments to add? (Examples of accomplishments include professional affiliations, languages you speak, certifications, licenses, **patents**, **publications**, honors, **awards**, and **volunteer work** you have done.)*

Who will be reading this résumé?

Am I being concise? (Can I say the same thing just as well using fewer words?)

Phrases for Seeking Résumé Assistance

Do you have time to _____ (read over / proofread / edit / work with me on) my résumé?

I would really value your feedback on my résumé.

I need help with this résumé. Do you _____ (feel comfortable helping / have the time to help / have some time this week to work with) me on this?

*How about a trade? If you will look over my résumé and give me some pointers, I will help you _____ (with your proposal / your budget report / set up that workshop). Thanks, in advance; I'm in a real **bind**. I need a job.*

Most résumés say "References Upon Request" at the bottom. You should not include the names or contact information for your **references** in your résumé, but carry this information with you so that you can give it to employers who ask for references. Always ask a person for permission before giving his or her name as a reference.

When you ask someone, either a teacher, a former employer, or a friend, to write a **letter of reference**, this is not an easy task. Give the person some time to do the job, and spend some time with your references to tell them about yourself, what kind of work you are looking for, and your past experience. Also, tell them what a potential employer needs to know about you. A teacher may be writing reference letters for many students; a former employer may be busy with a particular assignment, a planned business trip or vacation, or many other things; and a friend may even be looking for his or her own letters of reference. Keep in mind that you do not send the reference letters with the résumé, save them in a file for when you need them, so there is enough time for you to be **considerate** and/or **trade favors** with those you ask to write letters for you.

The Cover Letter

Each time you send your résumé, you should include a cover letter stating your interest in the company. The letter should not duplicate the information in your résumé, but it should briefly highlight the skills and positions you held previously that are appropriate to the position you seek. The cover letter can also be used to add information that you think might be important to the employer but is not on your résumé. Do the following in your cover letter:

- Demonstrate that you know something about the company you are applying to and that you are impressed by it. Not all applicants will do this; it's an **edge** that will get your application noticed.
- **Convey** enthusiasm about working for the company in this position.
- Be brief and to the point.
- Make sure grammar, spelling, and punctuation are correct. Proofread your letter carefully, and ask someone else to proofread it as well.
- Address the letter to the person you want to contact by name if possible, preferably the person who is doing the hiring.
- Print your letter on the same good quality paper as your résumé.

Helpful Cover Letter Hints

Create a standard letter that you **tailor** to each position.

What are the job qualifications? Do you have them?

What's required? How does your background reflect that you have the required skills, knowledge, or licenses?

What if your skills are "close, but not quite there"? Do you have skills in a similar area that are transferable? Do you learn quickly?

Two to three paragraphs, concise and well written, are sufficient for the body of your letter.

In the cover letter, you should state the specific position you are applying for, how you learned about it (or the name of the person who referred you), and how you are qualified. Briefly state what impresses you about the company and what you can contribute, stating your skill areas. Your final paragraph should refer the reader to your résumé for more detail and close with thanks for consideration and a request for action, such as an interview.

Phrases for the Cover Letter

I am applying for the position of _____ (front desk manager / floor supervisor / administrative assistant / bookkeeper).

I saw your ad in the . . .

I have worked on two continents for more than 20 years in the _____ (pharmaceutical / health-care / transportation / hospitality / utility) industry.

I was impressed to learn about your company's _____ (green initiative / environmental consciousness / community involvement / recent industry award).

I believe that my background in _____ (sales / service / technology / research) would make me a valuable part of your team.

Although I have not worked in the _____ (hospitality / telecommunications / textile / chemical) industry, I'm sure that my background and experience in _____ (public relations / human services / sales) is readily transferable.

Please note the relevant experience on my enclosed résumé.

Not included in my résumé, but valuable to this position, is my extensive volunteer experience teaching teens _____ (writing / customer service skills / sales / confidence building / entrepreneurship / team building).

Travel not only is not a problem for me, I enjoy meeting new people all the time.

I would appreciate the opportunity to meet with you to learn more about the position and discuss the contribution I can make to your company.

Idioms and Other Vocabulary

At the ready: available and prepared for immediate use

Awards: prizes given to recognize special service or achievements

Balancing act: trying to achieve two objectives equally without one diminishing the other; keeping two opposing sides evenly distributed

Bind: difficult place in life

Chronological résumé: a résumé that lists work experience in time order starting with the most recent and working back

Considerate: kind, thinking of others

Consistent: doing the same thing or having the same form throughout

Convey: tell about

Cover letter: a letter sent with a résumé that focuses on the particular position one is applying for

Created equal: in this case, the same identical résumé is sent out for every job

Curriculum vitae (CV): long and complete list of educational and work background sent when applying for an academic position

Delineate: carefully describe

Edge: advantage that no one else has

Functional résumé: a résumé that focuses on skills and experience

Letter of reference: letter written by a person familiar with you that describes your personal qualifications for employment

Not applicable (N/A): doesn't apply, has nothing to do with

Objective: goal, what kind of work you seek

One size doesn't fit all: the same résumé is not sent out for every position applied for, but changes are made to suit each specific position

On-site: at the place where you are given the application, in this case

Patents: document certifying a new invention (product or idea)

Pertain: have to do with

Publications: published writing

References: people who know you and can and will say or write positive things about you; employers may contact them to ask questions about you

Sell you: you are the "product" that you are selling or promoting

Tailor: to change, to make specifically right for

Trade favors: exchange of nice or kind things done for others

Unique: one of a kind

Volunteer work: good work done for no payment, helping people without being paid for it

Culture Hint: *The purpose of a résumé in the United States is to get you a face-to-face meeting or interview for the position you are seeking. Therefore, the emphasis is on clear and concise presentation of information. Additionally, the résumé has to be neat and easy to read, with no misspellings and other errors. Résumés are always keyboarded or typed using word processing software and a printer, never handwritten. No gimmicks such as dark-colored paper, unusual formatting, or hard-to-figure-out presentations should be used. Strategy is important; you want a well-planned set of steps to reach the end goal: getting a position, a job, work that suits you.*

Chapter 13

Job Interviews

An interview is just one of a number of methods available to an employer to select new employees. It is still the most widely used method. For many jobs, you may be interviewed more than once. The first interview, or **screening interview**, narrows the field to the most qualified candidates. Screening interviews tend to be short, and the questions asked are not usually highly technical, but concentrate more on the applicant's work history and motivation. The telephone interview is often used as a screening tool.

The **selection interview** is used to **probe** into the specific skills and abilities that may suit the candidate to the position. A selection interview may be conducted by one person, by a series of people one after the other, or by several people at once in what is called a panel interview. Some interviews take place over lunch or dinner.

Whether you are interviewing for a promotion or **lateral move** within your company or for a job with a new company, the same interviewing skills apply. The following tips will help you prepare for and succeed in the interview:

- Learn about the company before going for an interview.
- Check the company's Web page.
- Read about the company in company literature, business news, or industry reference books (a librarian can help you find this information).

- Think about how your skills and abilities suit you for the company and the job.
- Dress appropriately for the interview. Nice business attire is usually correct, except for certain jobs in which business attire is never worn. In these cases, wear clean, neat, casual clothes.
- Go with neat and clean hair, natural makeup, and **low-key** jewelry.
- Give your voice power by taking a few deep breaths, speaking with confidence, speaking slowly and clearly, and taking a warm drink rather than a cold one before your interview.

Here are some things to avoid doing in an interview:

- Do not **discredit** your present or previous employer.
- Do not **oversell** yourself by exaggerating your qualifications.
- Do not go to an interview with **scuffed** shoes, pantyhose or stockings with **runs**, **rumpled** or wrinkled clothes, dirty clothes, or body odor.
- Do not make any negative comments, such as remarking on the poor customer service skills of a company employee you noticed on your way in.
- Do not tell the "only slightly **off-color** but very funny" joke you recently heard.

Phrases That Describe What the Interviewer Will Do

Set the tone: The interviewer will attempt to put you at ease and will share general company and job information.

Elicit *information: The interviewer will ask you open-ended, behavioral questions such as "What would you do if . . . ?"*

Close the interview: The interviewer will thank you for your time and give you an idea of when you can expect to hear from the company.

A good idea, if you are going to interview at a company at which you really want to work and are not sure what to wear to the interview, is to drive to the company at the time work starts or at **quitting time** and park in front to observe the people coming in or going out. How are they dressed? (Don't choose **Casual Friday**!) Dress just a little better than this for the interview, as you are seeking to make a good first impression.

A good interviewer will ask open-ended questions, which tend to require more complete answers than just yes, no, or another short or one-word response. If the interviewer asks you closed questions, which lead to dead-end answers, you can add specific examples or further information to your answers to give yourself an opportunity to tell the interviewer more about your qualifications.

> **Open question:** What have you done that shows that you enjoy challenging work?
> **Closed question:** Do you enjoy challenging work?
> **Dead-end answer:** Yes, I do.
> **Open answer:** Yes. In my current position, for example, I coordinate all incoming requests and verify financial data. Often, I work within a very tight time frame.

Types of Interview Questions

Interviewers may ask **hypothetical** or behavioral questions to find out how you are likely to respond in a typical work situation. Here are some examples of hypothetical questions:

> *What would you do if . . . ?*

> *How would you respond to . . . ?*

Behavioral questions are similar, but for these you will describe what you have actually done in a work situation in the past. The following are behavioral questions:

What did you do in that situation?

What did you say?

Tell me about a time when . . . ?

The interviewer may also summarize what you have said. This provides you with an opportunity to add any missing or additional relevant information.

As I understand you, you're saying that . . .

Let me summarize.

Do you mind if I summarize?

The interviewer may also describe the position that is open and ask you a question like the following:

Tell me how your background and job expectations relate to what I've described.

Other Questions You Might Be Asked in an Interview

Are you good at motivating people?

How do you motivate people?

*Have you ever taken courses on your own to **further** your personal growth or education?*

What courses have you taken to further your growth or education?

Are you comfortable with change?

Can you give an example of how you've successfully handled change?

Do you handle stress well?

How do you handle stress?

Do you work well with others?

Tell me about an example of how you work well with others.

Phrases for Answering Twenty Common Interview Questions

Following are twenty questions that are often asked in job interviews, along with phrases and tips that will help you answer each one well.

1. Tell me about yourself.

I enjoy working, and also _____ (swimming / exercising / stamp or coin collecting / listening to music).

If your hobby is dangerous (like skydiving), this is not the time to mention it. If you had a long period of not working, address it with valid reasons and other things you did during that time.

I haven't worked for two years because _____ (I gave birth to twins and stayed home to care for them, and now I have a reliable nanny / I did some traveling / I wrote a book / I did volunteer training of at-risk youth, helping them earn their GEDs).

2. What special skills do you have that make you suited for this position?

Before the interview, study the requirements of the position you are interviewing for. In your answer, mention these requirements and describe your matching skills and experience.

3. Describe a recent situation when you had to use those skills.

Give details of a situation in one of your past jobs in which you successfully used the skills. You may be asked about clinical, scientific, mathematical, or people skills.

4. What was the most satisfying aspect of your most recent employment?

Be prepared to respond with information that highlights qualities the employer will value, such as the following:

I liked working together with a team to complete a difficult project.

5. How well acquainted are you with our company and its corporate structure?

Get acquainted with the company before the interview through the company Web site or brochures, media coverage, annual reports, etc., and respond with positive information you have learned about the company. Express how this knowledge affects your interest in working for the company.

I am aware that (company name) has been the top in its field for the past three years, and that you are expanding into new cities. I am excited about the possibility of being a part of this growth.

6. What major trends do you foresee for our industry in the next three to five years?

Do your homework before the interview: study industry forecasts so you can briefly demonstrate your knowledge of the industry.

7. Where do you see yourself, as far as work is concerned, in five years . . . ten years?

Learn the title of the person(s) interviewing you, and if the human resources (HR) director, for example, is interviewing you, you should never say, "I would like to be an HR director." Also, never say you'd like to be at a larger or smaller company, a company closer to home, or a company in another state. Instead, focus on the company where you are interviewing and say something like the following:

I see myself _____ (advancing here in this company / learning more about this company / bringing my new skills to this company).

8. Tell me about a time when you had to work with others to get a job done. What did you do?

Always give a positive example in which your team was successful.

I _____ (oversaw / worked with / worked under / cooperated with / was part of a team that) . . .

9. Describe a situation, either personal or professional, in which you had to overcome adversity. What did you do?

Again, this is an opportunity to highlight your skills and achievements.

*I _____ (finished within time **constraints** / supervised the repayment of bank debt / finished the project within budget / estimated costs accurately / quickly moved to **Plan B**).*

10. In your opinion, what attributes make for an ideal _____ (admin / project manager / production assistant)?

It's the job you are interviewing for, so find out the job requirements and match them with your qualifications in your answer.

11. Are you a team player?

Never respond to this question with "No." Give an example or details that support your "Yes" answer.

Yes, I enjoy working with others to accomplish a task cooperatively.

12. Would you prefer working alone?

This is a question for which answering either yes or no could be seen as negative, so it is best to give a more open answer like the following:

I also like the challenge of working alone, so it depends on the situation.

13. What is your greatest strength?

There's a fine line of distinction between answering this question well and bragging, so it's better to say something like,

"I learn quickly" instead of "I never make a mistake."

14 What is your greatest weakness?

The trick here is to turn a weakness into a strength, as in the following example.

Sometimes it takes me longer to accomplish a job because I am a perfectionist and I prefer to do a job well the first time rather than rushing through it and having to do it over.

15. Would you be able to relocate?

Think about this before the interview and answer honestly.

16. How far are you willing to travel?

This answer depends on the job and the times. It if is difficult to get work, you may consider traveling **farther**.

17. What made you select this career?

Your answer should show your fit for the position.

I've always _____ (been interested in / fascinated by / concerned with) _____ (computers / mathematical equations / science / helping people).

18. Describe a success in your professional or personal life and your part in making it a success.

*I was an **integral** part of increasing the company's sales budget by 50 percent.*

I created and controlled a streamlined budget.

I created Quality Control guidelines to add to existing ones.

19. What makes you angry?

How do you handle anger? Choose an example of something that angers most people, like hearing excuses instead of honest answers, and show how you manage your anger appropriately.

I _____ (confront the situation / talk it out / solve problems with others involved).

20. What are your Plans A and B for transportation to come to work?

Check out the public transportation to the job site before answering. "Know before you go." Driving may be A and public transportation may be B.

Questions to Ask in an Interview

The interviewer will most likely ask if you have any questions. You should have a few. Unless this meeting is one at which you are being hired, don't discuss salary or money or benefits yet. You should, however, do some research to learn the pay scale parameters of the field for when this does come up. Following are some good questions you might ask:

What will my duties be?

Where will I fit into _____ (the organization / the larger picture)?

To whom will I report and/or who will report to me?

What are the chances of advancement in this position?

Will traveling or relocation be required now or in the future?

What training does the company provide?

When will you decide on the appointment?

What is the next step?

Idioms and Other Vocabulary

Casual Friday: many companies allow employees to wear casual clothing on Fridays; also called Dress Down Friday

Constraints: limits

Discredit: make unfavorable comments about a person or organization

Elicit: ask for, draw out

Further: advance or increase

Hypothetical: based on an unreal but possible situation

Lateral move: a move to a different job, but on the same level within a company

Low-key: doesn't stand out, not flashy, quiet

Off-color: using unacceptable sexual language

Oversell: Praise yourself more than necessary

Plan B: your second plan which you can use if your first plan fails

Probe: question deeply, investigate

Quitting time: when work ends

Rumpled: looking like one slept in one's clothing

Runs: tears that run down a length of a stocking or hosiery

Screening interview: used to select candidates who are qualified for further interviews

Scuffed: worn away, scraped

Selection interview: beyond the screening interview, a more in-depth interview used to select a candidate or candidates for a final or job-offer interview

---

Culture Hints: In addition to "to do" rules for the interviewing process, there are also "don'ts"—things you should never to do at the interview.

- *Don't be late.*
- *Don't bring other people with you.*
- *Don't take notes during the interview; wait until afterward.*
- *Don't chew gum.*
- *Don't read your questions from a piece of paper; memorize them ahead of time.*
- *Don't interrupt the interviewer.*
- *Don't bring your cell phone, or turn it off and keep it out of sight.*
- *Don't pretend to know more than the interviewer; it won't impress him or her.*

Grammar Notes: *The words* further *and* farther *are used differently.* Further, *as a verb, means "to help something succeed or be achieved." Used as descriptive words (adverbs or adjectives),* farther *is used for distance and* further *to talk about amounts or quantities. For example, "I want to* further *my education" (verb). "I want to* further *study computers" (adverb). "If I take this job, I will work* farther *from my home than now" (adverb).*

Chapter 14

Follow-Up

Your follow-up might **seal the deal**. If not, it does show that you know professional courtesy, and even if you don't get this job, your résumé could end up in the "**keep in mind**" file.

Before you write a follow-up note or make a follow-up call, you might want to ask yourself some questions about the interview experience you just had.

Questions to Ask Yourself About the Interview

*Was I sufficiently **armed** with information about the job, the company, and the industry? If not, how can I improve on my research methods so I feel better prepared next time?*

*What did I forget, if anything, to say about myself that would better help me **sell myself** in the next interview? How can I insert this into a future interviewing conversation even if the interviewer doesn't ask a question that would bring it up? Can I do it without sounding like I'm **bragging**?*

What can I do to become less nervous before and during interviews?

What did I say that the interviewer _____ (seemed interested in / asked more questions about / followed up on / expressed a desire to talk about more)?

Do I really _____ (want to work / see myself / picture myself) in this _____ (environment / field / job / company / location)?

The appropriate follow-up can be a brief, handwritten thank-you note, a typed letter, or an e-mail. E-mail is fast and efficient and shows you are **at the top of your game**. Someone who is interviewing a variety of job candidates, however, might welcome one less item in his or her e-mail inbox and appreciate a letter that arrives with a stamp.

A follow-up phone call may be in order, especially if you are really interested in this job. You'll probably get voice mail and need to leave a message. Don't expect a return call; if the company is really interested in you, someone will call you. Write out your message first so you can deliver it clearly without **stumbling**. Always speak a bit more loudly and slowly when leaving a voice mail message. Some phones don't carry or receive them well.

Phrases for Follow-Up Letters or Messages

Thank you for taking time to speak with me today about the _____ (receptionist / factory / chemist / credit officer / administrative / supervisory / dispatcher) position.

I enjoyed learning about BBG Corporation and the _____ (receptionist / factory / chemist / credit officer / administrative / supervisory / dispatcher) job. I appreciated meeting so many members of the _____ (sales / production / human resources / art / advertising) department.

Please call me for _____ (answers to questions you may have / references / any additional information).

I would love to become part of the HHJ Team.

I look forward to hearing from you _____ *(after you complete the interviewing process / soon / next week).*

Thank you for meeting with me to discuss how my qualifications **mesh** *with the* _____ *(administrative / accounting / project coordinator / sales / production) position.*

The growth potential of this position is exciting.

I look forward to _____ *(joining WWM / having a second interview / the next stage of the interview process) in the near future.*

I found our conversation _____ **(stimulating / interesting / informative)**, *and hope that I have the opportunity to work with you.*

Idioms and Other Vocabulary

Armed: prepared
At the top of your game: knowing or being familiar with
  the most modern technology
Bragging: over-praising yourself
Juggling: keeping track of several things at once
Keep in mind: think about, remember
Mesh: go with or match
On the spot: immediately
On the spur of the moment: with no warning
Seal the deal: make sure of a positive outcome
Sell myself: make myself a most attractive candidate
Stimulating: filled with interesting ideas
Stumbling: making mistakes and unsure of one's words

Culture Hint: The telephone interview may be used as a first interview and a screening tool. This interview may occur **on the spur of the moment**. You might call a company to which you have sent a résumé to confirm receipt. Someone may then want to interview you **on the spot** over the telephone. The company may also set a time and date for a phone interview. In any case, be prepared.

- Have a pad and a pen handy.
- Have a mirror with you to check your smile. This idea will make you laugh before the call and relax your facial muscles. You won't sound sad or angry if you are smiling.
- A good trick is to have a copy of your résumé taped to a wall that you can see while on the phone.

Now, you are prepared: smiling, and not **juggling** a pad, a pen, and a résumé.

Part 3 Notes Section

Part 4

Participating in and Leading Meetings

"Opportunity Meets Preparation"

Gerhardt, a photographer, and Roberto, a **copywriter,** worked together for several years at a small **advertising agency.** The **writing was on the wall** at that agency; downsizing had been going on for almost a year and the agency would probably close in a few months.

Gerhardt and Roberto attended a meeting to present an **ad campaign** they had developed for the agency's biggest **client**. The meeting was at the client's office and the president of a large and **prestigious** ad agency was also in attendance. This larger agency would be taking over the client's account when the small agency **closed its doors**. Everyone was **on board** for this meeting: the new, well-known ad agency, the much smaller, soon-to-be-closed agency, and the client.

Gerhardt put his photographs up on a screen and Roberto supplied the words. They were a perfect team and after their presentation there was a **round of applause**. After the presentation, there were other issues on the agenda and during the coffee hour that followed, the president of the new ad agency approached Gerhardt and Roberto with an offer.

He wanted them to continue working on this client's account and, with the kind permission of the small agency's **board of directors**, join the new company for other work as well.

Chapter 15

Meeting Protocol and Etiquette

Meetings serve different purposes. Many meetings are scheduled regularly or ahead of time. Sometimes, an emergency or critical issue **pops up** and requires a **spur-of-the-moment** meeting. Some meetings are held strictly to share information that people need to know: department updates, company policy changes or initiatives, ongoing issues, and more. Other meetings are designed to solve problems or make decisions. These are usually more **interactive**.

Often, especially in manufacturing, transportation, and other industries in which many people must follow clearly stated assignments daily, managers or supervisors begin the day with a fast meeting to ensure that everyone is clear about his or her day's roles and responsibilities. These are not formal meetings, they are **quick hits** during which information is shared. These may be called morning meetings or **all hands meetings**.

Well-planned meetings serve everyone's needs. And whether you are leading a meeting or participating in one, your role is significant in terms of making the meeting productive for everyone.

A well-planned meeting has a defined purpose, is well led and managed, and includes a written agenda that is comprised of time frames, relevant background information, and clearly stated desired results. An effective meeting leader, or facilitator, begins on time, stays within stated **parameters**, and ends on time. He or she works to stay within the announced time frame, diplomatically controlling the flow of the discussion and discouraging **rambling**.

Effective meetings end; they do not **fade**, with people **randomly** leaving the room. The leader announces that the meeting will conclude and accepts final questions and/or comments. He or she then summarizes results, decisions, and actions to be taken. The facilitator then announces the next meeting date and thanks the participants.

Finally, the one who leads the meeting must distribute minutes and ensure that the **determined actions** are taken. Often, the facilitator **delegates** these tasks.

Meeting attendees should respect others by listening, acknowledging comments, not interrupting, and speaking politely.

Phrases for Meeting Protocol and Etiquette

Good _____ (morning / afternoon / evening).

*Thank you all for _____ (attending / coming **on short notice** / participating).*

We only have _____ (a half hour / an hour / two hours) to _____ (decide / explain / learn about / review) our _____ (direction / plans / recommendations / next steps).

Who would like to _____ (begin / take minutes)?

Who has a comment about . . . ?

What are your reactions to . . . ?

Miriam's suggestion is excellent. Thank you.

Excuse me, Roy, I believe Sherry wasn't finished. You can speak next.

I'd like to hear what Alice has been trying to say.

Let me just finish this thought before you comment.

Peter, as I understand, you agree with the intent but not the implementation plan.

Thank you.

Who's next? We only have ten minutes remaining.

Any questions at this point?

Let's summarize decisions and assigned tasks.

Can everyone make a follow-up meeting next Thursday?

Thank you all.

Idioms and Other Vocabulary

Ad campaign: ad is short for advertising, series of ads
All hands meetings: workplace meetings that everybody attends
Advertising agency: company that prepares ads
Board of Directors: governing body of a corporation
Break into: interrupt so one can be heard, because no one is pausing long enough for one to speak
Client: customer for a professional business
Closed its doors: shut down, went out of business
Copywriter: one who writes or edits written content
Delegates: assigns to people other than himself or herself
Determined actions: things to do that have already been decided on
Fade: gradually end instead of having a definite termination
Intimidating: making others too uncomfortable to say what they want to express
Interactive: working together

On board: included
On short notice: with no advance notification
Parameters: time or space borders or limits
Pops up: suddenly occurs
Prestigious: well-known, great reputation
Quick hit: fast, start-today, informative and informal
    meeting
Rambling: long, disorganized speaking
Randomly: happening without a plan
Reporting relationship: who reports to whom at work,
    who is subordinate to whom
Round of applause: clapping
Shout others down: raise your voice so loud that anyone
    else talking must stop and listen to you
Spur-of-the-moment: without warning or planning
Step in: to assume a role that isn't necessarily yours
    because the person with that responsibility isn't
    carrying it out
Unruly: not organized
Writing was on the wall: it was likely, almost certain
    that something would take place, usually something
    negative

Culture Hint: *Every culture has its own protocol for meetings.*
Although this chapter describes the ideal meeting in the United
States, the reality varies among states, regions, companies, and
within companies. Many people regularly interrupt others. This
can not only become annoying, but to people from cultures that
more strictly adhere to the rules, this behavior can be **intimidat-**
ing. *Others raise their voices for a number of reasons. They may*
be frustrated by the content of the discussion or their inability to
break into *the conversation. Some just choose to* **shout others**
down. *A good facilitator will control these disruptions. Some-*

times the facilitator doesn't have the skills needed to control an **unruly** *meeting participant. Occasionally, someone who is not running the meeting has to* **step in** *and say, "Can we please hear from Ben?" or "Harry, we hear you. Now give someone else a chance to respond." All of this depends a lot on the working and* **reporting relationships** *among those in the group.*

Chapter 16

Brainstorming and Decision-Making Meetings

Often, a team must make decisions about direction, opportunities, crises, unexpected events, and more.

The most useful approach to problem solving and decision making is an organized one. Many groups use a **brainstorming** process: Everyone **tosses out** ideas without weighing their merit. Then the group decides which ideas to consider and why. Once the choices have been **narrowed down**, they can be explored in **further** detail, with the group examining the positive and negative consequences of each path. Once a solution is agreed upon, the group discusses specific steps to implement the solution. Sometimes a problem requires a **multipronged** solution. This is a simple overview. Lively discussion and debate is key to the process.

Phrases

*Let's get everyone's thoughts **on the table**.*

All ideas are valuable. Don't hold back.

*Henry, could you write these ideas on the **flip chart**, please?*

Excuse me; this is not the time for debate.

Let's keep going.

*That's a little **way out**, but it could work. I like it.*

Let's look at this idea another way.

Now, which of these can we _____ (eliminate / throw out / do away with)?

Let's put these ideas into categories.

Let's go through these ideas and sort what we have.

What goes together?

Let's build on that idea.

We've narrowed our options down to . . .

Consider which would probably be the most _____ (workable / appealing to our manager / budget-worthy / doable / efficient / effective).

What does everyone think?

Roberta, I haven't heard from you yet—what do you think?

*Okay, let's **run it up the flagpole**.*

*That's an interesting **digression**, but we have to wrap this up by three o'clock.*

*I didn't **catch** what you said. Could you repeat it?*

*Let's stay focused; no _____ (**tangents** / side conversations / **censoring** of ideas).*

I'm sorry. I don't _____ (understand what you mean / know those words in English / understand that saying). Could

117

you please _____ (explain that to me / say that in other words / let me use my dictionary)?

I have only _____ (been in the United States for six months / studied English for six months), and this is my first brainstorming meeting.

Idioms and Other Vocabulary

Acronym: a word consisting of the first letters of words or a phrase e.g., IRA (Individual Retirement Account)

Brainstorming: free expression of all ideas

Catch: get, understand, hear everything

Censoring: suppressing, repressing

Digression: movement away from the main topic

Flip chart: large tablet of paper on an easel used for casual brainstorming and taking notes during a meeting

Further: beyond already stated (see the "Grammar Notes" sidebar in Chapter 13)

Multipronged: many parts (a fork has a number of prongs)

Narrowed down: selected from a large group

On the table: out for all to see or hear

Pick up on: be sensitive to, understand, become familiar with

Run it up the flagpole: test or try an idea; entire idiomatic quote is "run it up the flagpole and see if anybody salutes"

Tangent: topic other than the topic being discussed

Tosses out: offers ideas

Vantage point: different position or way of thinking

Way out: not conventional, unusual

Culture Hint: When cultures come together at meetings—probably especially at brainstorming meetings—speaking and understanding styles may clash. It often takes longer for you as a foreign-born person to process information when many people are speaking—sometimes at the same time. Many times, those new to the United States like yourself are translating in their heads as they go along. Therefore, you may not catch everything in a brainstorming meeting as soon as it is said, making it difficult to interject a point. Americans use many idioms, inexact grammatical constructions, and **acronyms**. Normally, you would look these up, ask someone about them, or otherwise find out "what's going on." There is no time for this during a brainstorming meeting. After a lively meeting, you might make this comment: "Before I could say what I wanted to say, the group was onto the next topic."

As the purpose of a brainstorming meeting is to generate new ideas and strategies, it is crucial that all participants get a chance to participate—especially those from other cultures or **vantage points**.

A sensitive facilitator may recognize the challenge for those who find it difficult to keep up and may pull those who seem to be trying to speak, or those who haven't had a chance to speak yet, into the conversation. If the appointed facilitator doesn't **pick up on** what is happening, as a member of the group you can intervene instead. One technique is saying, for example, "Here's what I think about . . ."

Chapter 17

Team and Department Meetings

Team and department meetings are often regularly scheduled meetings with **tight agendas**. A team may be charged with initiating and completing a specific project or with ongoing responsibilities for certain tasks. Teams may be within a department or **cross-functional**. Department meetings often center around the department's mission, goals, and activities. Sometimes meetings are called to share information so that **the left hand knows what the right hand is doing**. Other company meetings are the quick hit meetings described in the introduction to this chapter.

Phrases for Team and Department Meetings

This meeting should last a half hour.

I've allocated specific times on the agenda for each team report. Please try to stay within your time frame.

*This morning's meeting for the maintenance **crew** will be only ten minutes.*

Can we have brief team reports?

*Please use the flip chart if you haven't put your key points on **PowerPoint** slides. Some of us are visual.*

Since our last meeting, a number of changes have taken place in the department.

My _____ (project / report / responsibility / group) is continuing on schedule.

Please explain how our department can have a stronger working relationship with _____ (sales / service / manufacturing / finance / operations).

The following people are assigned to _____ (the lobby / the factory / the restrooms).

*Does everyone have a **full complement** of supplies?*

We will distribute additional supplies at the end of this meeting.

*I am afraid that the _____ (new project / scheduling system / **breakdown** of teams) has created _____ (a **bottleneck** / an objection from management / an unacceptable **deadlock**).*

Thank you, everyone.

Idioms and Other Vocabulary

Bottleneck: a blockage, a slowdown, a deterrent to progress

Breakdown: arrangement of the teams, members of the team

Crew: team of workers

Cross-functional: involving more than one department

Deadlock: standstill, decision cannot be reached, agreement cannot be made

121

Full complement: all the supplies required to perform the task

Loosen up: feel more comfortable, relax, become more expressive

PowerPoint: a popular software program that enables the user to present ideas in a series of slides

The left hand knows what the right hand is doing: improve communication so all who are working together know what each other is doing

Tight agendas: strict meeting rules that allow no tangents or rambling

---

Culture Hint: *Sometimes a culture lesson changes a person's outlook or entire way of behaving. For example, Ahn, a slot cashier at a major casino hotel, attended a company-sponsored English as a second language (ESL) program that I coordinated. Ahn was a lovely, quiet, shy Vietnamese woman. She came to class visibly upset one day when I happened to be observing. "What's wrong, Ahn?" Ahn's teacher and I asked. Ahn was upset because she had received a poor performance evaluation. Her supervisor informed her that many customers/guests complained that Ahn did not readily offer to help them, rarely smiled, and spoke so softly that they couldn't hear her. "In my country," Ahn explained, "I was taught to be shy, quiet, and look down when speaking. That is respectful in my country. Also, the casino is noisy, and it is very hard for me to raise my voice enough to be heard." "We'll have to work on that," I replied.*

The teacher and I developed a plan for Ahn to speak into a tape recorder using customer service phrases such as, "Hello," "Good afternoon," "Good evening," "You seem lost," "May I help you?" "May I direct you?" and others.

At first, Ahn spoke into the recorder in her normal voice. We listened, and of course, couldn't hear her. We turned up the

volume louder, and Ahn's voice sounded normal to us and more understandable. Ahn covered her ears and responded, "I sound angry." Little by little, we practiced with the tape recorder, and soon, without it. Ahn spoke across a classroom trying to make herself understood, and finally, she practiced on the casino floor. She also practiced smiling and learned why approaching customers is not considered rude in America. Ahn began to **loosen up** *and enjoyed her new volume. When I next visited the class, a smiling Ahn was the center of attention. She had just received an excellent performance evaluation and was loudly expressing her joy and relief.*

Chapter 18

Teleconferencing, Videoconferencing, and Webinars

With people within companies working worldwide and companies working within a global market, **face-to-face** meetings are far from the only option. Teleconferencing has long been an avenue for including off-site meeting participants or for coordinating a group of people who just can't all get to the same place at the same time. Teleconferencing allows any number of people at different locations to communicate with each other at a time set up in advance.

Videoconferencing changed long-distance communication by allowing people at different locations to participate in discussions and/or meetings through the use of interactive video. The geometric changes in technology in recent years have led to less expensive, more efficient face-to-face interactions through the Internet. This latest advance, which many use at home to visit friends and relatives with the click of a mouse, allows colleagues and business associates to have discussions as though they were in the same room.

Online learning is available in many forms as well, the latest being the webinar, which allows participants to view the same material online and discuss it.

The important steps in making arrangements for all of these technology-driven innovations are to confirm that each participant has the essential equipment and that time differences in the various locations have been checked and the scheduled times are convenient for all.

If you're new to a language, participating in a teleconference may be intimidating. Without seeing the participants' faces, you can't pick up on their facial clues as to how your points are being taken. The small talk that usually precedes a meeting may feel awkward in a teleconference. Attaching voices to names may be difficult. (You can help with this problem by repeating your own name when you make a point.) And speaking so that you can be heard may feel as if you are shouting. After a teleconference call, get some feedback from your colleagues about your participation.

Phrases for Teleconferencing—Planning

Are you free for an hour conference call of the Strategic Planning Committee on Monday at 1 P.M.?

Please find out the best time for an hour conference call.

Scheduling a call at 1 P.M. accommodates all United States time zones.

I'm on the road, but I can call in on my cell phone.

*Willy is recovering from the flu and won't be in for our staff meeting. His input is **crucial**. Let's call and have him join us by phone. Don't forget to hit "speaker."*

What about Tom? He's _____ (on a business trip in Spain / vacationing in Egypt but wants to join us / is interviewing a possible new associate in the Hong Kong office).

Dial 800-543-9876 to reach the conference operator.

Phrases for Teleconferencing

The Strategic Planning Committee representatives from our four locations need to resolve some key issues.

Please say your name and location so we know that everyone is here.

Hi, this is Harry from Purchasing in Chicago.

So, Howard, what's the weather like in Santa Fe today? We're freezing in Michigan.

*We have one hour for this conference, so let's _____ (**stay on track** / keep to the schedule / save **chitchat** for the end).*

This is Marie, I'd like to bring up . . .

Jen here, I would want to know . . .

Let's assure that this action goes forward. Does anyone disagree?

We've covered our complete agenda in 50 minutes.

Thank you all. I'll e-mail a summary of our discussion to all of you.

Phrases for Videoconferencing—Planning

Does your office have videoconferencing equipment?

What does it cost to rent videoconferencing equipment?

We have a small conference room that would accommodate videoconferencing.

I like videoconferencing rather than teleconferencing because we can see _____ (facial expressions / body language / visuals / posters).

Please have the visuals we discussed ready for the videoconference.

*Please confirm the time and purpose of the Friday morning videoconference before I **sign off on** our occupying that conference room.*

Find out what size PC monitors are available. I'd like the largest possible.

We can also set up several PCs and have each participant from our site use one.

Don't forget your laptop. You're going to have to conference in for that meeting even though you'll be off site.

Please wear _____ (a jacket and tie / conservative clothing / the company logo shirt) tomorrow. We're going to meet our newest client's sales team via computer conference at 2 P.M.

Phrases for Videoconferencing

*Please speak up. Voices don't always **carry** as well as we'd expect.*

Good morning, Shannon. You look great today.

It's a pleasure to see your faces today.

Am I looking at _____ (snow / sleet / heavy rain / fog / the sun shining) through the window behind you?

We put together some visuals to better explain our proposal.

*Do you want a _____ (short break / coffee break / lunch break)? We can **reconvene** in about ten minutes.*

Phrases for Webinars

A webinar on using our new computer software program will be offered on Tuesday at 10 A.M. EST and one hour earlier at 9 A.M. CST. A makeup session is scheduled for Friday at the same times.

To sign in, use the code SW.

If you would like to complement your participation with a telephone component, please call 888-487-2845.

You will be able to print out the help screens to have them available for review or reference.

We will offer a series of training webinars next month.

Could we have a brief orientation about how to participate in a webinar before the first one is scheduled?

Idioms and Other Vocabulary

Carry: reach to a distance, be easily heard
Chitchat: small talk, conversation, side conversation
Crucial: critical, important, decisive
Face-to-face: personally, in each other's presence
Reconvene: meet again, pick up where one left off
Sign off on: approve, agree on
Stay on track: continue on the same topic, in one
    direction until finished
Venture out: take a chance going where you may not be
    comfortable
Venue: place where people go to participate in activities

---

*Culture Hint: A webinar is a good way to conduct or sit in on a meeting or take a class without leaving your home or office until you are confident enough to **venture out** to other **venues**. Webinars have become very popular in the United States and are offered on just about any subject.*

Part 4 Notes Section

_____

_____

_____

_____

_____

_____

_____

_____

_____

_____

_____

_____

_____

_____

_____

_____

_____

Part 5

Professional Development

"Look Up Bullheaded in the Dictionary"

An advanced ESL student from India returned to his tutoring sessions after a hospital stay. He chose to discuss the hospital stay and his questions, concerns, and fears about his stay and about health care in general with his tutor. He talked about the intravenous (he pronounced it "in-TRAV-en-ous") treatments he received during his stay. The tutor corrected his pronunciation by saying that in the United States we say "in-tra-VEN-ous," not "in-TRAV-en-ous." The student was shocked and insisted his pronunciation was correct in the United States. The tutor used this as a **jumping-off point** for discussing how one can use the dictionary, not only to learn the meaning of a word, but also to learn the pronunciation as well. The tutor went to the dictionary and said, "Let's look it up." The student was **eager** to do so and prove himself correct. They looked the word up in the dictionary and saw that the tutor had given the student correct advice. The shocked student decided that he wanted to check other dictionaries in the room and, finally, his own small pocket American English dictionary. All of them showed the same pronunciation. The student looked up at his tutor and said, "Well, I like my way better!" He continued to talk about his hospital stay to others, using his preferred pronunciation, and was constantly questioned about the word *intravenous*. Perhaps he should have looked up the word **stubborn**.

Chapter 19

Self-Evaluation

Professional development is an ongoing process that begins before you even **land** your first job and continues throughout your career. Feedback is an important element of professional development. Everyone wants to know how he or she is doing. Employees, coworkers, and even bosses want to know how they are doing and how they can improve.

A first step in the process is self-evaluation, taking a good look at your strengths and **shortcomings** so you know what you need to improve. Other **components** are feedback to and from others, job coaching, and performance evaluations. All of these are tools that give you information about what you are doing well and what you need to strengthen. Then, you need to look at how to build on your strengths and enhance those areas that are not **up to par**.

Self-evaluation means looking carefully at yourself in your work environment. What are your strengths, things you do well? What holds you back or is difficult for you? The easiest way to evaluate yourself is to think about how an employer might evaluate you. He or she would look at your **interpersonal** and communication **skills**, your specific job skills, and technical and nontechnical skills related to your work and your job. When you evaluate yourself, think about these areas.

Think about the words that describe what makes you a valuable employee. If you are evaluating yourself to determine how you can demonstrate your value to your current employer or a prospective employer, think about verbs that describe your accomplishments.

By evaluating yourself, you focus on things that you do well and the characteristics that define you. Just as you want to look in the mirror before leaving for work to ensure that you look your best—do your socks match, is your shirt buttoned correctly, or is your lipstick on your teeth—you want to get a good look at your skills and behaviors before someone else **scrutinizes** them.

Phrases for Self-Evaluation—Questions to Ask Yourself

Do I enjoy my work?

What do I enjoy about my work?

Do I like working with others?

Am I more effective when I work alone?

*When someone makes a suggestion, am I **open to** it?*

Do I find myself losing my temper or trying not to lose my temper when others make mistakes?

Do I become upset when I make mistakes?

Do I blame others for my mistakes?

Am I comfortable taking responsibility for my mistakes?

Can I accept corrections without feeling uncomfortable?

Do I sometimes wish that I could _____ (speak / write / calculate / solve problems / plan / organize) better?

Have others suggested that I could _____ (speak / write / calculate / solve problems / plan / organize) better?

Do others seek my _____ (advice / assistance / input / opinion)?

Does or do my _____ (foreman / supervisor / manager / boss / coworkers / subordinates) speak well of my work?

What _____ (skills / knowledge) would I like to strengthen?

What skills do I have that are adaptable or transferable?

What qualities do I have that help me succeed?

What talents or abilities do I have that are valuable for this job? Other jobs?

Why am I an **asset** to _____ (this company / my boss)?

Phrases That Describe What You Have Accomplished

I edited _____ (a company newsletter / the monthly bulletin / all my department's reports).

I reduced _____ (my department's budget by 12 percent / absenteeism in the company to half / the number of reams of paper we order by using scrap paper).

I created a process for _____ (**tracking** expenses / improving product quality / cutting down on employee overtime).

I conducted a number of _____ (training programs / PowerPoint courses / employee surveys that were published).

I am an **asset** to this company because . . .

I have made improvements in . . .

Words that I believe describe me: _____ .

Accurate   Dependable
Calm   Hardworking
Cooperative   **Loyal**

Words I would like to add to words that describe me: _____

Adaptable   **Versatile**
Flexible   **Confident**

Idioms and Other Vocabulary

Adaptable: able to change according to the situation
Asset: someone or something that is valuable
Big: important, popular
Bullheaded: won't change one's mind even though shown that one is being unreasonable
Calm: relaxed
Components: parts that make up the whole
Confident: sure of oneself
Eager: having a strong desire
Flexible: able to adapt or change direction as needed
Interpersonal skills: skills for dealing with people
Jumping-off point: a point at which to start
Land: are hired for; get
Loyal: true to, trustworthy
Open: receptive, willing to listen and consider using an idea
Scrutinize: look at very carefully
Shortcomings: faults, lacks
Stubborn: won't change one's mind even though shown that one is being unreasonable
Touchy-feely: negative word for courses that deal with feelings and emotions instead of information or action

Tracking: keeping track of, a process for seeing how
    something is being done, such as money being spent
Up to par: at the required standard
Versatile: able to do many different things

Culture Hint: *Introspection and self-evaluation are **big** in the*
United States. There are many books, online programs, and
courses in this area. Courses or training programs may even be
offered in your company. Sometimes these programs are referred
*to as **touchy-feely** courses as opposed to courses that deal with*
information and/or action such as statistics, classical music
appreciation, and language courses.

Chapter 20

Giving and Accepting Feedback

Giving and accepting feedback are activities that make many people uncomfortable. They have difficulty finding the right words and the right time to tell a coworker or employee that he or she is **falling short**. In order to be useful, feedback must be heard and considered or processed. Following some simple rules can make it easier for others to accept your feedback. Base the feedback on facts rather than perceptions, make it clear and specific, and provide it in an amount the receiver can **handle** (a **digestible** amount). Ensure that the feedback is useful by directing it at an action or behavior that the receiver can change.

While most people are comfortable praising others or giving positive feedback, almost everyone is uncomfortable receiving or accepting praise. The easiest way to accept praise is to say, "Thank you" or "I appreciate your noticing." Many of us, however, try to **deflect** the praise by **minimizing** the behavior for which we are being praised.

Giving Feedback

The best way to give constructive or developmental feedback to help someone improve his or her job performance is to focus on job-related behavior and avoid generalities and **labels**. Use specific examples so the person understands what should be changed. For example, you might tell someone, "Your work has been late a number of times" rather than labeling him or her by saying, "You are inefficient." And always give this feedback in private. Receiving developmental feedback or correction is difficult to begin with. Don't make matters worse by giving it in front of others so that it embarrasses the person.

Giving Feedback Phrases—Praise

Thank you for that extra effort! You made the entire team shine!

*I would love to have you participate in a new project we're **launching**.*

Almost all of your clients have written letters praising you. Congratulations.

Apex appreciates your quality service.

Shawn, I am grateful for your dependability. You are always on time, and I can always count on your getting the job done efficiently and well.

*Kiesha, your smile **epitomizes** the word pleasant. You _____ (say good morning / communicate well with everyone / smile and make eye contact).*

*Rashid, your _____ (enthusiasm / commitment to our company / attention to detail) not only shows in your work but also is **contagious**.*

*Ana, your _____ (taking on new projects / generating creative ideas / keeping everyone **in the loop**) has positively **affected** your entire team.*

I appreciate the constructive ideas that you offered at today's meeting, Mike.

This is a thorough and well-written proposal.

Your efficiency is a real asset in reorganizing the department.

Giving Feedback Phrases—
Constructive Criticism

Yes, working on a team can be frustrating. You do have to adjust to others' styles. What do you think you can do to make it less frustrating?

I appreciate your editing my work, but I cannot read your suggestions. They are always valuable to me; please try to write more clearly.

Can we review the sections of the report that you contributed? Some are unclear to me, and others seem to be missing information.

I understand that you have ongoing car problems; however, I have a business to run. You must be on time for your shift. What alternative, reliable transportation is available to you?

*Safety is our number one priority. Please do not **take** our safety procedures and equipment rules **lightly**.*

*Myra, I acknowledge your **diligence**. Perhaps this accordion file can help you organize **as you go**, rather than having to spend extra time each morning before you start work.*

Mary, we seem to keep showing up to use the conference room at the same time. Are you aware that there's a schedule for the conference room at the receptionist's desk? If we both write down our meeting times, we can be sure of when the room is available.

I couldn't help overhearing your conversation with Dan because you were raising your voice. You might want to be more aware of this in the future.

Jean, you may not be aware of the tone you used when speaking to that customer. I'm sure you'd want to know that it made you sound uninterested. I know that's not true.

*Rob, we've talked about your manner in communicating with your coworkers. Shouting at **anyone** in the workplace is unacceptable. I'm afraid this is your final warning. Please don't **force** me to take **next steps**.*

(In a business environment, once someone has been told to change the way he or she is doing a job, if that person does not change, a next step might be a formal warning, followed by suspension or firing if the person still does not do what is required.)

Accepting Feedback

Accepting developmental feedback **graciously** is the mark of a professional person interested in doing his or her best at work. Some people may not be as **tactful** as they should be, but don't **kill the messenger**. Listen to the real message. Ask questions for clarification. For example, if a colleague says that you are rude, the comment itself is rude and **insensitive**. It is not helpful because it does not tell you what you are doing that the person does not like. Still, find out why he or she said it. Ask, "What did I do that makes you say that?" You may be surprised by the answer. It could be things such as not making eye contact, raising your voice, or an **unintentional snub** that you can change if you are aware that the person perceives them as being rude.

Accepting Feedback Phrases

*How do you think I should **address** that problem?*

Now I understand that I should have come to you with that information. In the future, I'll know what to do. Thank you.

*Thank you for letting me know that some of my coworkers think that I don't reach out to them or make myself accessible. My lack of English skills makes me shy, but I am taking ESL classes. I'll work on smiling more and saying hello. I know that is part of our **corporate culture**.*

Sometimes I'm so focused on my work that I don't even notice when someone stops by my desk. Sorry I didn't see you.

*Yes, I know I've been late more than three times in the past two weeks. Someone suddenly dropped out of our **car pool**. That's all **worked out** now. It won't happen again.*

I didn't realize that I had raised my voice to the client on the phone. I was becoming frustrated, but I know I can't let that show. I'll be more careful.

*My intention was not to "boss" Sheila. I was trying to help her out. I guess I have to work on my **style**.*

*I'm concerned that John thinks that I **stole** his client. I would never do that. Let me explain what happened.*

I realize that my computer skills need improvement. Can you recommend a course?

*Thank you for _____ (offering me the opportunity to take the ESL course / suggesting that I take advantage of **flextime** / advising me to check on the earlier bus / letting me know about the company day-care center for Anna).*

I appreciate your giving me the information on _____ (ESL classes / technical training / anger management training).

Idioms and Other Vocabulary

Address: face, handle, do something about

Affected: caused change to

As you go: little by little as you do the work, not at the beginning or the end of a job

Car pool: arrangement for people going to the same place to travel together in one car; the verb for this is *carpool*

Contagious: something that gets others involved, they see someone's enthusiasm and they become enthusiastic also

Corporate culture: a combination of behaviors and expectations practiced and held by people in a particular company

Deflect: redirect, turn aside; in this context, to dismiss as not true or unimportant

Diligence: giving focused attention and working hard

Digestible: in small pieces and easily taken and applied

Epitomizes: is the perfect example of

Falling short: not meeting expectations, not doing your job as well as one should

Flextime: working a set number of hours, but starting and/or finishing when it is convenient for the employee

Force: make it necessary for someone to do something; insist on someone doing something

Graciously: appreciatively

Handle: accept

Insensitive: not thinking about others' feelings

In the loop: informed

Kill the messenger: get angry with someone who is giving you information

Labels: a word, usually unflattering, used to describe someone

Launching: starting off for the first time

Minimizing: making less of, treating as unimportant

Next steps: those actions that follow a current action in a procedure or plan

Stole: took without permission; past tense of *steal*

Style: manner in which one does or says things

Tactful: careful not to hurt or embarrass others

Take lightly: not pay careful attention to

Unintentional snub: appearing to ignore someone when one did not intend to do so, such as not acknowledging the person's presence because one is focused on something else and does not notice that the person is there

Worked out: taken care of, fixed to everyone's satisfaction

Culture Hints: *The two most frequently used forms of feedback are developmental or constructive feedback and positive feedback. Both types of feedback only work well when they are focused on specific behaviors. Saying, "Your rudeness is unacceptable" does not help the employee understand what behaviors are considered rude. Two people who come from different cultures may have different ideas on what is rude or polite, but if the feedback describes the specific behaviors that are causing the person to be seen as rude, he or she will be able to make the changes that are needed.*

The most important aspects of giving and accepting feedback are listening skills and communication skills.

Chapter 21

Job Coaching

Whether you are the owner or manager of a small business or have a management or supervisory position within a large company, ongoing coaching of your employees is one of your most significant responsibilities. By letting people know what you expect and giving ongoing feedback, you strengthen your team. Sometimes the feedback is not enough and an employee needs a concentrated coaching session that focuses on what he or she needs to change, why, and by when. Coaching also needs to focus on how. How will the employee change, and how can you help?

Coaching is an expanded form of developmental feedback. Use the guidelines in Chapter 20 for focusing on behavior and giving clear examples. Always give the employee the opportunity to solve his or her problem before you jump in with a solution.

Phrases for Job Coaching

Let's set aside a time to discuss this more fully.

Your presentation skills have improved greatly. You spoke clearly and confidently yesterday.

*During the past two months, your **output** has slipped dramatically. Is everything okay? How can I help you **get back on track**?*

*Kebria, you have not attended any of your **personal improvement plan (PIP)** training sessions. Can you explain why?*

*I know that the economy is difficult and work is stressful, but spending time complaining is unproductive and **demoralizing** for others. Can you **redirect** that energy? We would all appreciate it.*

What will you do to prevent this in the future?

*Juanita, we've talked before about checking facts before including them in our _____ (company literature / newsletter / monthly memo to clients / weekly blog). What is your process? What can you do to **tighten** it?*

Sonia, I notice that you've been taking extended lunch hours. This is not acceptable. Is there a problem we should discuss? Please let me know about any need for _____ (a longer lunch time / a late arrival / an early departure) to address a specific problem.

Victor, you spend a lot of time on your computer with little to show for it. I'm concerned that you may be spending that time using your computer for personal reasons that interfere with your work. If you are involved with computer games, personal e-mail, or social networking, these are not allowed. If you are not, we have to discuss what is slowing you down so much.

*Your **tardiness** affects _____ (others on your team / your customer retention efforts / my ability to start the day with a quick meeting). Is there an explanation? If there's a problem, it must be solved. If there isn't one, you have to make a greater effort. This is not acceptable.*

I understand that you have a challenge working out transportation. The HR department has bus schedules as well as a list of employees looking to carpool. Let's talk next Tuesday to see how you're resolving the problem.

Warren, you will be giving more presentations to other departments during the next few months. I've noticed that when you speak before a group, you _____ (don't make eye contact / drop your voice at the ends of sentences / become **defensive** *when asked a question / rock back and forth /* **jiggle** *the change in your pocket). These are all things that you can easily change with the right help. I'd like you to attend the Development Track course on Presentation Skills. You'd be surprised at the major effect that a few changes will have.*

Sue, a number of customers have complained that you don't approach them to offer help and that when you do, you don't speak clearly and loudly. Are you uncomfortable approaching customers? What do you think would help?

Yes, I think a customer service course is a great idea. You might also want to **keep an eye on** *Norman. He's very comfortable in that role. Notice how he handles it.*

Idioms and Other Vocabulary

Change course: go in a different direction

Defensive: reacting by defending oneself or criticizing the person asking the question rather than just answering it politely

Demoralizing: negatively affecting the morale or spirit of someone

Get back on track: get back to doing things the way you did before you became ineffective or distracted

Jiggle: shake; jiggling coins in one's pocket makes a distracting noise

Keep an eye on: watch, see how someone does something

Move on: go on to better opportunities

Outgrow: become more skilled, more competent, and more knowledgeable than the job requires

Output: the amount of work that someone gets done

Personal improvement plan (PIP): a plan that employer and employee work on together to help the employee overcome problems at work and/or improve skills and knowledge; may include courses, monitoring of work, a mentor, and recommendations for behavior changes

Redirect: investing in something else

Tardiness: being late

Tighten: make the process stronger so that errors don't slip by

*Culture Hint: Job coaching has become an important part of the workplace in the United States and other countries. The reason for coaching someone on the job is the same as the reason for coaching an athlete in a sport. You want that person to do the best job possible. A good manager wants his or her employees to be so good that they **outgrow** their jobs and get promotions and **move on**. A good coach does not wait until the employee has done a lot of things wrong, made a lot of errors, or is doing very poorly to take action. He or she talks to the employee before the employee faces serious problems. If someone is late once or twice, the employer can watch and wait, but by the third time, a problem is evident and a coaching session is in order. Some problems require immediate action, such as when an employee raises his or her voice to a coworker or a customer. That is a behavior that must not be repeated. An immediate coaching session is also needed if an employee ignores a safety regulation. The role of the coach is not to embarrass or humiliate the employee, but to find out what is wrong and help the employee **change course**.*

Chapter 22

Performance Evaluation Meetings

Coaching and feedback are part of the ongoing process of performance evaluation. This process provides the employee and employer with a **framework** for support, encouragement, **reinforcement**, and correction.

The performance evaluation meeting is at a scheduled time. Both the employer and the employee—usually a manager or supervisor and the worker who reports to him or her—prepare for this meeting throughout the year. Each should document both positive and negative work-related events, behaviors, and issues. This discussion should not be an unprepared talk about the employee's recent behavior only.

Performance Evaluation Phrases— Outstanding Performance

Meets and exceeds set goals and objectives _____ (enthusiastically / professionally / competently).

Requests additional responsibilities.

Assists others readily.

Outstanding _____ (creative / mathematics / writing / editing / speaking) skills.

Takes initiative.

Trains others in . . .

Completes all work _____ (on time / early / within budget / under budget / error free / efficiently).

Provides _____ (unasked for assistance / coverage for others / **unsolicited** information).

Works well independently.

Effective team player.

Performance Evaluation Phrases— Exceeds Expectations

Initiates new projects.

Creates solutions.

Requests _____ (explanations / additional duties).

Meets all goals and objectives, exceeds some.

Takes most assigned tasks to the **next level**.

Accepts responsibility.

Requests additional training or coaching when needed.

Diligently completes PIP training and more.

Performance Evaluation Phrases— Meets Expectations

Meets most goals and objectives.

Completes assignments on time.

Catches and corrects errors.

Works well with minimal supervision.

Graciously accepts feedback.

Offers suggestions.

Communicates clearly.

Successfully follows recommendations of PIP.

Performance Evaluation Phrases— Needs Improvement

Does not adequately meet all goals and objectives.

Not readily accepting of criticism.

Does not follow directions.

Does not arrive on time.

Poor _____ (communication / math / production line / sales / telephone / speaking / writing) skills.

Spends too much time _____ (organizing / reorganizing / reviewing / setting up / double checking).

Occasionally submits _____ (incomplete / inaccurate / sloppy) work.

Clients and customers occasionally complain about _____ (rudeness / inaccuracies / incomplete orders / lack of attention).

Performance Evaluation Phrases— Communication

Regularly reports on progress.

Participates in department meetings.

Always confirms appointments.

Asks relevant questions.

Listens carefully without interrupting.

Performance Evaluation Phrases— Team Building

Works effectively within department.

Reaches out to counterparts in other departments.

Gives credit to coworkers.

Offers to help others.

Performance Evaluation Phrases—Initiative

Frequently requests additional responsibility.

*Is not **timid** about offering suggestions to coworkers or managers.*

Always proofreads outgoing correspondence without being asked.

*Offers to stay late when he or she observes a coworker or supervisor is **under the gun**.*

Phrases for a Sample Evaluation Discussion—Employer

Let's review your annual goals and objectives and how you've met them.

Your initiative on our recent _____ (sales project / store opening / client retentions program) is impressive. I like the way you stepped in to ensure that everyone was working toward the same goal.

*You started the year with some problems _____ (car trouble / tardiness / misunderstandings with a coworker / losing a major account / a safety **infraction**).*

*I'm glad that you stepped up to the plate and resolved (that / those) issue(s). That's **commendable**.*

*You've met and exceeded all of your goals except for _____ (your **target** for increased sales / adding to your client **portfolio** / achieving a customer service award / writing a training component / creatively cutting your project expenses). What are your thoughts on that?*

Yes, it is _____ (a tough market / an increasingly changing demographic / a technically changing environment / a challenging team environment / a new direction). What are you doing differently to overcome that?

Great . . .

You've met all of your performance improvement training goals.

How has that worked for you?

What is your personal objective for the coming year?

May I see the draft plan you've developed?

This is ambitious, but I have every confidence in you.

So, let's summarize . . .

I've enjoyed this discussion. Keep up the good work.

Phrases for a Sample Evaluation—Employee

I enjoyed _____ (leading the team during the product **rollout** / working on the XM project / teaming up with IT for a joint project / learning about high-level customer service techniques / attending ESL classes / completing the foreman training program).

I really appreciated your patience during _____ (my childcare crisis / my recent health problem / my car pool disaster / my error on the capital request). I'm glad to be back on track.

Meeting my goals was a challenge, but one that I enjoyed.

I'm frustrated by not _____ (achieving my sales quota / being able to get through on the phone to some key customers). I welcome suggestions.

The courses that I attended were extremely helpful.

I know that my _____ (customer service skills / computer skills / writing skills / grammar skills / English language skills / meeting management skills) could be improved. What do you suggest?

Here is a draft of my goals for the coming year. Are they **in line with** your expectations?

Thank you for listening so well and for your useful feedback and suggestions.

Idioms and Other Vocabulary

Commendable: deserving of praise
Diligently: carefully
Framework: structure or system of organization
Infraction: the act of breaking a rule

In line with: the same as, similar to, in agreement with
Next level: the next step beyond the current one, further
Portfolio: in this case, a list of active clients or customers
Reinforcement: strengthening, stimulation
Rollout: introduction of a product; the verb for introducing a product is *roll out*
Sloppy: not carefully done
Takes initiative: goes ahead and does what needs to be done without waiting to be asked
Target: what one wants to reach or achieve
Timid: shy, scared
Under the gun: under a lot of pressure to complete a task
Unsolicited: not asked for

Culture Hint: Often in the United States, a company will have you evaluate yourself before you report to your performance evaluation. This is a good idea because it allows you to see how closely your self-evaluation matches your supervisor's evaluation of your work. Additionally, if you disagree with your supervisor's evaluation, the self-evaluation process will have given you time to think about an appropriate response. Even if your company does not require you to do a self-evaluation, you may choose to evaluate yourself on your own for this reason.

Chapter 23

Resources for Professional Development

Once you've learned what you do well and what you can do better, think about all of the resources available to you. Even those areas that are your strongest can be made still stronger, **positioning** you to be a leader in your field, your job, or a particular skill.

Many **options** are available for **accessing** the help you need. First are the **do-it-yourself** routes. These include reading about skills to gain specific knowledge as well as taking online or computer-based courses that you either enroll in yourself, get from the library, or access through your workplace.

Other options include people or training programs that are available to you through your company. Find a mentor at work, someone who has the skills and knowledge that you require and is willing to help you learn. Ask about on-the-job training programs (OJT) within your company. These are programs that train you to become **proficient** at the job while you are doing it. Also ask your supervisor if your company offers any training courses. Many companies have training departments and offer courses **in-house**. Others send employees **off-site** for skill development. Many combine both routes to employee improvement.

Phrases for Accessing Professional Development Resources

I am eager to improve my _____ (English / customer service / technical / financial / communication / writing skills). Is there a company library? I'd like to start by reading about this.

I know that I can do better with _____ (customer service / conflict resolution / stress management / writing skills). Do we have online courses available?

I would like to work toward a promotion. Can you recommend any off-site courses in supervisory or management skills?

*I heard that the local community college has courses specifically for our industry in _____ (grant writing / taxation / insurance / foreign exchange). Is **tuition reimbursement** available for that?*

I noticed in our training catalog that courses will be offered in _____ (basic writing / advanced writing / technical writing / credit writing / scientific writing). Do I need to be recommended for a course or can I just register?

I'd like to take some college courses in _____ (human resources planning / strategic planning / community planning / English / accounting / Spanish). Are they covered by our tuition reimbursement program? Do you agree that they would be helpful?

*I belong to an organization for _____ (accountants / printers / internal public relations staff / government agency managers / industry professionals). I'd like to attend the national conference in **D.C.** Do you think that would be possible?*

I'm trying to improve my team leadership skills. Do you mind mentoring me? I've always had an interest in your field.

*I'd like to be assigned to the strategic planning team. Can you suggest a training course to _____ (**get my feet wet** / give me some background / help prepare me)?*

I know that in my evaluation you rated me "meets expectations" in presentation skills. Do you think _____ (I could do better with some help / an advanced course might help me become even better / joining Toastmasters would give me more practice)?

*Although my sales are beyond my target, I think I could do better if I were more computer **savvy**. So much is happening online these days. Is there a course you know of?*

*I missed the beginning of the three-week service training; it began during my disability leave. Can I **pick it up** now, or should I wait for the next **cycle**?*

I have a lot of related experience and would love to have a chance at OJT for _____ (manufacturing line manager / front desk service representative).

Idioms and Other Vocabulary

Accessing: getting to

Cycle: a complete series or sequence

D.C.: District of Columbia; Washington, D.C., is the capital of the United States

Do-it-yourself: doing something on your own rather than getting help from others

Get my feet wet: get acquainted with

In-house: within the company

Off-site: at a location other than the company

Options: choices

Pick it up: catch up

Positioning: putting in a place

Proficient: good at

Savvy: have practical knowledge about

Tuition reimbursement: a process by which an employee pays for a course and the company pays him or her back, often after the course is completed

Culture Hint: *There are two major locations named Washington in the United States, so if someone refers to "Washington," it is important to know which place he or she means. Washington, D.C., is independent of any state and is the capital of the United States. It is located between Maryland and Virginia near the eastern coast of the United States. The state of Washington is in the northwest corner of the United States. Its capital city is Olympia, and its largest city is Seattle.*

Part 5 Notes Section

_____

_____

_____

_____

_____

_____

_____

_____

_____

_____

_____

_____

_____

_____

_____

_____

Appendix

Self-Confidence and Selling Yourself **in a Nutshell**

There is a common expression, "You never get a second chance to make a first impression." This, of course, is true. But you do have a chance to change that first impression. Sometimes you just **sense** that something about you could be improved. There are ways to see and hear yourself as others do. Look at yourself on video, in a **candid photo** in action, in a full-length mirror, and **facially**, in a magnifying mirror. What looks good? Why? What doesn't look as good? Change it! Check your smile, your eye contact, and your image in your mirror and in the photos. Ask for honest advice from a close friend or a relative whom you trust.

Listen to your voice. Record yourself in conversation, making a short presentation, and reading. Is your voice too soft, timid, or scared sounding? Is it too loud, **frantic**, or **pushy**? Is it too slow, **monotonous**, or boring? Is it too fast, nervous, or difficult to understand? Ask others to listen to your voice and give you feedback.

What about your handshake? Is it firm but not **bone-crushing**? Is it **limp** or **tentative**? What about your **wardrobe**? What about **grooming**? What about **posture**?

Once you appraise yourself in any or all of these ways, think about your successes, both professional and personal, and your part in making them successful. While you are in that success **frame of mind**, practice phrases such as the following (depending on the kind of work you do).

Phrases to Reinforce Self-Confidence

I made a strong presentation to my department today.

The boss was impressed with my customer service skills.

I placed Pablo in a good job today.

*I (got two **listings** / opened eleven new checking accounts / signed up my tenth customer).*

*I sold a piece of property no one else could **unload**.*

Stavros appreciates my English lessons.

I feel more at ease in front of a group of people now.

Idioms and Other Vocabulary

Bone-crushing: very strong, so strong or hard it could almost crush or break the bones in one's hand

Candid photo: a photograph taken when the subject isn't aware that it is being taken

Facially: having to do with the face

Frame of mind: attitude or mood

Frantic: very worried and nervous and in a panicked state of mind

Grooming: taking care of one's hair, body, and clothing in a neat, clean way

In a nutshell: presenting the main ideas clearly and concisely

Limp: weak

Listings: real estate, personnel, and some other businesses sign deals to hire, sell, etc.; getting clients this way is called getting listings

Monotonous: of unvarying tone, boring

Posture: position of the body, how it is held

Pushy: overly forceful in a negative way

Sense: to have a feeling, instinct

Tentative: not definite

Unload: get rid of, sell, or give away something no longer wanted or needed

Wardrobe: clothing you have

Culture Hint: *Living in an individualistic society, Americans value self-confidence in order to sell themselves. There is a saying, "Everyone sells." Areas in which this quality is most evident include applying for work, moving up in work, selling and buying anything at the best price, negotiating for anything, and meeting people in business or in personal life. Self-confidence is a valued behavior in the United States.*

163

About the Author

Natalie Gast brings more than 30 years' experience to language training. In 1986, she founded Customized Language Skills Training (CLST), a full-service language training company specializing in tailor-made, short- and long-term English as a second language (ESL) and accent reduction programs on-site in business and industry. Additionally, CLST conducts training in many foreign languages.

CLST has developed industry-specific programs for foreign medical residents, engineers, bank management personnel, casino personnel, and employees of many other industries.

Gast earned her undergraduate degree at Boston University, and her master's degree work was done at Kean College, New Jersey. She has participated in conferences on responding to the changing economy, doing business with foreign countries, and workplace diversity. *Perfect Phrases for ESL: Advancing Your Career* is the companion volume to *Perfect Phrases for ESL: Everyday Business Life*.

The Right Phrase for Every Situation...Every Time

Perfect Phrases for Building Strong Teams
Perfect Phrases for Business Letters
Perfect Phrases for Business Proposals and Business Plans
Perfect Phrases for Business School Acceptance
Perfect Phrases for College Application Essays
Perfect Phrases for Cover Letters
Perfect Phrases for Customer Service
Perfect Phrases for Dealing with Difficult People
Perfect Phrases for Dealing with Difficult Situations at Work
Perfect Phrases for Documenting Employee Performance Problems
Perfect Phrases for Executive Presentations
Perfect Phrases for Landlords and Property Managers
Perfect Phrases for Law School Acceptance
Perfect Phrases for Lead Generation
Perfect Phrases for Managers and Supervisors
Perfect Phrases for Managing Your Small Business
Perfect Phrases for Medical School Acceptance
Perfect Phrases for Meetings
Perfect Phrases for Motivating and Rewarding Employees
Perfect Phrases for Negotiating Salary & Job Offers
Perfect Phrases for Perfect Hiring
Perfect Phrases for the Perfect Interview
Perfect Phrases for Performance Reviews
Perfect Phrases for Real Estate Agents & Brokers
Perfect Phrases for Resumes
Perfect Phrases for Sales and Marketing Copy
Perfect Phrases for the Sales Call
Perfect Phrases for Setting Performance Goals
Perfect Phrases for Small Business Owners
Perfect Phrases for the TOEFL Speaking and Writing Sections
Perfect Phrases for Writing Grant Proposals
Perfect Phrases in American Sign Language for Beginners
Perfect Phrases in French for Confident Travel
Perfect Phrases in German for Confident Travel
Perfect Phrases in Italian for Confident Travel
Perfect Phrases in Spanish for Confident Travel to Mexico
Perfect Phrases in Spanish for Construction
Perfect Phrases in Spanish for Gardening and Landscaping
Perfect Phrases in Spanish for Household Maintenance and Child Care
Perfect Phrases in Spanish for Restaurant and Hotel Industries

Visit mhprofessional.com/perfectphrases for a complete product listing.

Learn more. Do more.